A Discourse Upon The Origin And The Foundation Of The Inequality Among Mankind

By Jean Jacques Rousseau

INTRODUCTORY NOTE

Jean Jacques Rousseau was born at Geneva, June 28, 1712, the son of a watchmaker of French origin. His education was irregular, and though he tried many professions--including engraving, music, and teaching--he found it difficult to support himself in any of them. The discovery of his talent as a writer came with the winning of a prize offered by the Academy of Dijon for a discourse on the question, "Whether the progress of the sciences and of letters has tended to corrupt or to elevate morals." He argued so brilliantly that the tendency of civilization was degrading that he became at once famous. The discourse here printed on the causes of inequality among men was written in a similar competition.

He now concentrated his powers upon literature, producing two novels, "La Nouvelle Heloise," the forerunner and parent of endless sentimental and picturesque fictions; and "Emile, ou l'Education," a work which has had enormous influence on the theory and practise of pedagogy down to our own time and in which the Savoyard Vicar appears, who is used as the mouthpiece for Rousseau's own religious ideas. "Le Contrat Social" (1762) elaborated the doctrine of the discourse on inequality. Both historically and philosophically it is unsound; but it was the chief literary source of the enthusiasm for liberty, fraternity, and equality, which inspired the leaders of the French Revolution, and its effects passed far beyond France.

His most famous work, the "Confessions," was published after his death. This book is a mine of information as to his life, but it is far from trustworthy; and the picture it gives of the author's personality and conduct, though painted in such a way as to make it absorbingly interesting, is often unpleasing in the highest degree. But it is one of the great autobiographies of the world.

During Rousseau's later years he was the victim of the delusion of persecution; and although he was protected by a succession of good friends, he came to distrust and quarrel with each in turn. He died at Ermenonville, near Paris, July 2, 1778, the most widely influential French writer of his age.

The Savoyard Vicar and his "Profession of Faith" are introduced into "Emile" not, according to the author, because he wishes to exhibit his principles as those which should be taught, but to give an example of the way in which religious matters should be discussed with the young. Nevertheless, it is universally recognized that these opinions are Rousseau's own, and represent in short form his characteristic attitude toward religious belief. The Vicar himself is believed to combine the traits of two Savoyard priests whom Rousseau knew in his youth. The more important was the Abbe Gaime, whom he had known at Turin; the other, the Abbe Gatier, who had taught him at Annecy.

QUESTION PROPOSED BY THE ACADEMY OF DIJON

What is the Origin of the Inequality among Mankind; and whether such Inequality is authorized by the Law of Nature?

A DISCOURSE UPON THE ORIGIN AND THE FOUNDATION OF THE INEQUALITY AMONG MANKIND

'Tis of man I am to speak; and the very question, in answer to which I am to speak of him, sufficiently informs me that I am going to speak to men; for to those alone, who are not afraid of honouring truth, it belongs to propose discussions of this kind. I shall therefore maintain with confidence the cause of mankind before the sages, who invite me to stand up in its defence; and I shall think myself happy, if I can but behave in a manner not unworthy of my subject and of my judges.

I conceive two species of inequality among men; one which I call natural, or physical inequality, because it is established by nature, and consists in the difference of age, health, bodily strength, and the qualities of the mind, or of the soul; the other which may be termed moral, or political inequality, because it depends on a kind of convention, and is established, or at least authorized, by the common consent of mankind. This species of inequality consists in the different privileges, which some men enjoy, to the prejudice of others, such as that of being richer, more honoured, more powerful, and even that of exacting obedience from them.

It were absurd to ask, what is the cause of natural inequality, seeing the bare definition of natural inequality answers the question: it would be more absurd still to enquire, if there might not be some essential connection between the two species of inequality, as it would be asking, in other words, if those who command are necessarily better men than those who obey; and if strength of body or of mind, wisdom or virtue are always to be found in individuals, in the same proportion with power, or riches: a question, fit perhaps to be discussed by slaves in the hearing of their masters, but unbecoming free and reasonable beings in quest of truth.

What therefore is precisely the subject of this discourse? It is to point out, in the progress of things, that moment, when, right taking place of violence, nature became subject to law; to display that chain of surprising events, in consequence of which the strong submitted to serve the weak, and the people to purchase imaginary ease, at the expense of real happiness.

The philosophers, who have examined the foundations of society, have, every one of them, perceived the necessity of tracing it back to a state of nature, but not one of them has ever arrived there. Some of them have not scrupled to attribute to man in that state the ideas of justice and injustice, without troubling their heads to prove, that he really must have had such ideas, or even that such ideas were useful to him: others have spoken of the natural right of every man to keep what belongs to him, without letting us know what they meant by the word belong; others, without further ceremony ascribing to the strongest an authority over the weakest, have immediately struck out government, without thinking of the time requisite for men to form any notion of the things signified by the words authority and government. All of them, in fine, constantly harping on wants, avidity, oppression, desires and pride, have transferred to the state of nature ideas picked up in the bosom of society. In speaking of savages they described citizens. Nay, few of our own writers seem to have so much as doubted, that a state of nature did once actually exit; though it plainly appears by Sacred History, that even the first man, immediately furnished as he was by God himself with both instructions and precepts, never lived in that state, and that, if we give to the books of Moses that credit which every Christian philosopher ought to give to them, we must deny that, even before the deluge, such a state ever existed among men, unless they fell into it by some extraordinary event: a paradox very difficult to maintain, and altogether impossible to prove.

Let us begin therefore, by laying aside facts, for they do not affect the question. The researches, in which we may engage on this occasion, are not to be taken for historical truths, but merely as hypothetical and conditional reasonings, fitter to illustrate the nature of things, than to show their true origin, like those systems, which our naturalists daily make of the formation of the world. Religion commands us to believe, that men, having been drawn by God himself out of a state of nature, are unequal, because it is his pleasure they should be so; but religion does not forbid us to draw conjectures solely from the nature of man, considered in itself, and from that of the beings which surround him, concerning the fate of mankind, had they been left to themselves. This is then the question I am to answer, the question I propose to examine in the present discourse. As mankind in general have an interest in my subject, I shall endeavour to use a language suitable to all nations; or rather, forgetting the circumstances of time and place in order to think of nothing but the men I speak to, I shall suppose myself in the Lyceum of Athens, repeating the lessons of my masters before the Platos and the Xenocrates of that famous seat of philosophy as my judges, and in presence of the whole human species as my audience.

O man, whatever country you may belong to, whatever your opinions may be, attend to my words; you shall hear your history such as I think I have read it, not in books composed by those like you, for they are liars, but in the book of nature which never lies. All that I shall repeat after her, must be true, without any intermixture of falsehood, but where I may happen, without intending it, to introduce my own conceits. The times I am going to speak of are very remote. How much you are changed from what you once were! 'Tis in a manner the life of your species that I am going to write, from the qualities which you have received, and which your education and your habits could deprave, but could not destroy. There is, I am sensible, an age at which every individual of you would choose to stop; and you will look out for the age at which, had you your wish, your species had stopped. Uneasy at your present condition for reasons which threaten your unhappy posterity with still greater uneasiness, you will perhaps wish it were in your power to go back; and this sentiment ought to be considered, as the panegyric of your first parents, the condemnation of your contemporaries, and a source of terror to all those who may have the misfortune of succeeding you.

DISCOURSE FIRST PART

However important it may be, in order to form a proper judgment of the natural state of man, to consider him from his origin, and to examine him, as it were, in the first embryo of the species; I shall not attempt to trace his organization through its successive approaches to perfection: I shall not stop to examine in the animal system what he might have been in the beginning, to become at last what he actually is; I shall not inquire whether, as Aristotle thinks, his neglected nails were no better at first than crooked talons; whether his whole body was not, bear-like, thick covered with rough hair;

and whether, walking upon all-fours, his eyes, directed to the earth, and confined to a horizon of a few paces extent, did not at once point out the nature and limits of his ideas. I could only form vague, and almost imaginary, conjectures on this subject. Comparative anatomy has not as yet been sufficiently improved; neither have the observations of natural philosophy been sufficiently ascertained, to establish upon such foundations the basis of a solid system. For this reason, without having recourse to the supernatural informations with which we have been favoured on this head, or paying any attention to the changes, that must have happened in the conformation of the interior and exterior parts of man's body, in proportion as he applied his members to new purposes, and took to new aliments, I shall suppose his conformation to have always been, what we now behold it; that he always walked on two feet, made the same use of his hands that we do of ours, extended his looks over the whole face of nature, and measured with his eyes the vast extent of the heavens.

If I strip this being, thus constituted, of all the supernatural gifts which he may have received, and of all the artificial faculties, which we could not have acquired but by slow degrees; if I consider him, in a word, such as he must have issued from the hands of nature; I see an animal less strong than some, and less active than others, but, upon the whole, the most advantageously organized of any; I see him satisfying the calls of hunger under the first oak, and those of thirst at the first rivulet; I see him laying himself down to sleep at the foot of the same tree that afforded him his meal; and behold, this done, all his wants are completely supplied.

The earth left to its own natural fertility and covered with immense woods, that no hatchet ever disfigured, offers at every step food and shelter to every species of animals. Men, dispersed among them, observe and imitate their industry, and thus rise to the instinct of beasts; with this advantage, that, whereas every species of beasts is confined to one peculiar instinct, man, who perhaps has not any that particularly belongs to him, appropriates to himself those of all other animals, and lives equally upon most of the different aliments, which they only divide among themselves; a circumstance which qualifies him to find his subsistence, with more ease than any of them.

Men, accustomed from their infancy to the inclemency of the weather, and to the rigour of the different seasons; inured to fatigue, and obliged to defend, naked and without arms, their life and their prey against the other wild inhabitants of the forest, or at least to avoid their fury by flight, acquire a robust and almost unalterable habit of body; the children, bringing with them into the world the excellent constitution of their parents, and strengthening it by the same exercises that first produced it, attain by this means all the vigour that the human frame is capable of. Nature treats them exactly in the same manner that Sparta treated the children of her citizens; those who come well formed into the world she renders strong and robust, and destroys all the rest; differing in this respect from our societies, in which the state, by permitting children to become burdensome to their parents, murders them all without distinction, even in the wombs of their mothers.

The body being the only instrument that savage man is acquainted with, he employs it to different uses, of which ours, for want of practice, are incapable; and we may thank our industry for the loss of that strength and agility, which necessity obliges him to acquire. Had he a hatchet, would his hand so easily snap off from an oak so stout a branch? Had he a sling, would it dart a stone to so great a distance? Had he a ladder, would he run so nimbly up a tree? Had he a horse, would he with such swiftness shoot along the plain? Give civilized man but time to gather about him all his machines, and no doubt he will be an overmatch for the savage: but if you have a mind to see a contest still more unequal, place them naked and unarmed one opposite to the other; and you will soon discover the advantage there is in perpetually having all our forces at our disposal, in being constantly prepared against all events, and in always carrying ourselves, as it were, whole and entire about us.

Hobbes would have it that man is naturally void of fear, and always intent upon attacking and fighting. An illustrious philosopher thinks on the contrary, and Cumberland and Puffendorff likewise affirm it, that nothing is more fearful than man in a state of nature, that he is always in a tremble, and ready to fly at the first motion he perceives, at the first noise that strikes his ears. This, indeed, may be very true in regard to objects with which he is not acquainted; and I make no doubt of his being terrified at every new sight that presents itself, as often as he cannot distinguish the physical good and evil which he may expect from it, nor compare his forces with the dangers he has to encounter; circumstances that seldom occur in a state of nature, where all things proceed in so uniform a manner, and the face of the earth is not liable to those sudden and continual changes occasioned in it by the passions and inconstancies of collected bodies. But savage man living among other animals without any society or fixed habitation, and finding himself early under a necessity of measuring his strength with theirs, soon makes a comparison between both, and finding that he surpasses them more in address, than they surpass him in strength, he learns not to be any longer in dread of them. Turn out a bear or a wolf against a sturdy, active, resolute savage, (and this they all are,) provided with stones and a good stick; and you will soon find that the danger is at least equal on both sides, and that after several trials of this kind, wild beasts, who are not fond of attacking each other, will not be very fond of attacking man, whom they have found every whit as wild as themselves. As to animals who have really more strength than man has address, he is, in regard to them, what other weaker species are, who find means to subsist notwithstanding; he has even this great advantage over such weaker species, that being equally fleet with them, and finding on every tree an almost inviolable asylum, he is always at liberty to take it or leave it, as he likes best, and of course to fight or to fly, whichever is most agreeable to him. To this we may add that no animal naturally makes war upon man, except in the case of self-defence or extreme hunger; nor ever expresses against him any of these violent antipathies, which seem to indicate that some particular species are intended by nature for the food of others.

But there are other more formidable enemies, and against which man is not provided with the same means of defence; I mean natural infirmities, infancy, old age, and sickness of every kind, melancholy proofs of our weakness, whereof the two first are common to all animals, and the last chiefly attends man living in a state of society. It is even observable in regard to infancy, that the mother being able to carry her child about with her, wherever she goes, can perform the duty of a nurse with a great deal less trouble, than the females of many other animals, who are obliged to be constantly going and coming with no small labour and fatigue, one way to look out for their own subsistence, and another to suckle and feed their young ones. True it is that, if the woman happens to perish, her child is exposed to the greatest danger of perishing with her; but this danger is common to a hundred other species, whose young ones require a great deal of time to be able to provide for themselves; and if our infancy is longer than theirs, our life is longer likewise; so that, in this respect too, all things are in a manner equal; not but that there are other rules concerning the duration of the first age of life, and the number of the young of man and other animals, but they do not belong to my subject. With old men, who stir and perspire but little, the demand for food diminishes with their abilities to provide it; and as a savage life would exempt them from the gout and the rheumatism, and old age is of all ills that which human assistance is least capable of alleviating, they would at last go off, without its being perceived by others that they ceased to exist, and almost without perceiving it themselves.

In regard to sickness, I shall not repeat the vain and false declamations made use of to discredit medicine by most men, while they enjoy their health; I shall only ask if there are any solid observations from which we may conclude that in those countries where the healing art is most neglected, the mean duration of man's life is shorter than in those where it is most cultivated? And how is it possible this should be the case, if we inflict more diseases upon ourselves than medicine can supply us with remedies! The extreme inequalities in the manner of living of the several classes of mankind, the excess of idleness in some, and of labour in others, the facility of irritating and satisfying our sensuality and our appetites, the too exquisite and out of the way aliments of the rich, which fill them with fiery juices, and bring on indigestions, the unwholesome food of the poor, of which even, bad as it is, they very often fall short, and the want of which tempts them, every opportunity that offers, to eat greedily and overload their stomachs; watchings, excesses of every kind, immoderate transports of all the passions, fatigues, waste of spirits, in a word, the numberless pains and anxieties annexed to every condition, and which the mind of man is constantly a prey to; these are the fatal proofs that most of our ills are of our own making, and that we might have avoided them all by adhering to the simple, uniform and solitary way of life prescribed to us by nature. Allowing that nature intended we should always enjoy good health, I dare almost affirm that a state of reflection is a state against nature, and that the man who meditates is a depraved animal. We need only call to mind the good constitution of savages, of those at least whom we have not destroyed by our strong liquors; we need only reflect, that they are strangers to almost every disease, except those occasioned by wounds and old age, to be in a manner convinced that the history of human diseases might be easily composed by pursuing that of civil societies. Such at least was the opinion of Plato, who concluded from certain remedies made use of or approved by Podalyrus and Macaon at the Siege of Troy, that several disorders, which these remedies were found to bring on in his days, were not known among men at that remote period.

Man therefore, in a state of nature where there are so few sources of sickness, can have no great occasion for physic, and still less for physicians; neither is the human species more to be pitied in this respect, than any other species of animals. Ask those who make hunting their recreation or business, if in their excursions they meet with many sick or feeble animals. They meet with many carrying the marks of considerable wounds, that have been perfectly well healed and closed up; with many, whose bones formerly broken, and whose limbs almost torn off, have completely knit and united, without any other surgeon but time, any other regimen but their usual way of living, and whose cures were not the less perfect for their not having been tortured with incisions, poisoned with drugs, or worn out by diet and abstinence. In a word, however useful medicine well administered may be to us who live in a state of society, it is still past doubt, that if, on the one hand, the sick savage, destitute of help, has nothing to hope from nature, on the other, he has nothing to fear but from his disease; a circumstance, which oftens renders his situation preferable to ours.

Let us therefore beware of confounding savage man with the men, whom we daily see and converse with. Nature behaves towards all animals left to her care with a predilection, that seems to prove how jealous she is of that prerogative. The horse, the cat, the bull, nay the ass itself, have generally a higher stature, and always a more robust constitution, more vigour, more strength and courage in their forests than in our houses; they lose half these advantages by becoming domestic animals; it looks as if all our attention to treat them kindly, and to feed them well, served only to bastardize them. It is thus with man himself. In proportion as he becomes sociable and a slave to others, he becomes weak, fearful, mean-spirited, and his soft and effeminate way of living at once completes the enervation of his strength and of his courage. We may add, that there must be still a wider difference between man and man in a savage and domestic condition, than between beast and beast; for as men and beasts have been treated alike by nature, all the conveniences with which men indulge themselves more than they do the beasts tamed by them, are so many particular causes which make them degenerate more sensibly.

Nakedness therefore, the want of houses, and of all these unnecessaries, which we consider as so very necessary, are not such mighty evils in respect to these primitive men, and much less still any obstacle to their preservation. Their skins, it is true, are destitute of hair; but then they have no occasion for any such covering in warm climates; and in cold climates they soon learn to apply to that use those of the animals they have conquered; they have but two feet to run with, but they have two hands to defend themselves with, and provide for all their wants; it costs them perhaps a great deal of time and trouble to make their children walk, but the mothers carry them with ease; an advantage not granted to other species of animals, with whom the mother, when pursued, is obliged to abandon her young ones, or regulate her steps by theirs. In short, unless we admit those singular and fortuitous concurrences of circumstances, which I shall speak of hereafter, and which, it is very possible, may never have existed, it is evident, in every state of the question, that the man, who first made himself clothes and built himself a cabin, supplied himself with things which he did not much want, since he had lived without them till then; and why should he not have been able to support in his riper years, the same kind of life, which he had supported from his infancy?

Alone, idle, and always surrounded with danger, savage man must be fond of sleep, and sleep lightly like other animals, who think but little, and may, in a manner, be said to sleep all the time they do not think: self-preservation being almost his only concern, he must exercise those faculties most, which are most serviceable in attacking and in defending, whether to subdue his prey, or to prevent his becoming that of other animals: those organs, on the contrary, which softness and sensuality can alone improve, must remain in a state of rudeness, utterly incompatible with all manner of delicacy; and as his senses are divided on this point, his touch and his taste must be extremely coarse and blunt; his sight, his hearing, and his smelling equally subtle: such is the animal state in general, and accordingly if we may believe travellers, it is that of most savage nations. We must not therefore be surprised, that the Hottentots of the Cape of Good Hope, distinguish with their naked eyes ships on the ocean, at as great a distance as the Dutch can discern them with their glasses; nor that the savages of America should have tracked the Spaniards with their noses, to as great a degree of exactness, as the best dogs could have done; nor that all these barbarous nations support nakedness without pain, use such large quantities of Piemento to give their food a relish, and drink like water the strongest liquors of Europe.

As yet I have considered man merely in his physical capacity; let us now endeavour to examine him in a metaphysical and moral light.

I can discover nothing in any mere animal but an ingenious machine, to which nature has given senses to wind itself up, and guard, to a certain degree, against everything that might destroy or disorder it. I perceive the very same things in the human machine, with this difference, that nature alone operates in all the operations of the beast, whereas man, as a free agent, has a share in his. One chooses by instinct; the other by an act of liberty; for which reason the beast cannot deviate from the rules that have been prescribed to it, even in cases where such deviation might be useful, and man often deviates from the rules laid down for him to his prejudice. Thus a pigeon would starve near a dish of the best flesh-meat, and a cat on a heap of fruit or corn, though both might very well support life with the food which they thus disdain, did they but bethink themselves to make a trial of it: it is in this manner dissolute men run into excesses, which bring on fevers and death itself; because the mind depraves the senses, and when nature ceases to speak, the will still continues to dictate.

All animals must be allowed to have ideas, since all animals have senses; they even combine their ideas to a certain degree, and, in this respect, it is only the difference of such degree, that constitutes the difference between man and beast: some philosophers have even advanced, that there is a greater difference between some men and some others, than between some men and some beasts; it is not therefore so much the understanding that constitutes, among animals, the specifical distinction of man, as his quality of a free agent. Nature speaks to all animals, and beasts obey her voice. Man feels the same impression, but he at the same time perceives that he is free to resist or to acquiesce; and it is in the consciousness of this liberty, that the spirituality of his soul chiefly appears: for natural philosophy explains, in some measure, the mechanism of the senses and the formation of ideas; but in the power of willing, or rather of choosing, and in the consciousness of this power, nothing can be discovered but acts, that are purely spiritual, and cannot be accounted for by the laws of mechanics.

But though the difficulties, in which all these questions are involved, should leave some room to dispute on this difference between man and beast, there is another very specific quality that distinguishes them, and a quality which will admit of no dispute; this is the faculty of improvement; a faculty which, as circumstances offer, successively unfolds all the other faculties, and resides among us not only in the species, but in the individuals that compose it; whereas a beast is, at the end of some months, all he ever will be during the rest of his life; and his species, at the end of a thousand years, precisely what it was the first year of that long period. Why is man alone subject to dotage? Is it not, because he thus returns to his primitive condition? And because, while the beast, which has acquired nothing and has likewise nothing to lose, continues always in possession of his instinct, man, losing by old age, or by accident, all the acquisitions he had made in consequence of his perfectibility, thus falls back even lower than beasts themselves? It would be a melancholy necessity for us to be obliged to allow, that this distinctive and almost unlimited faculty is the source of all man's misfortunes; that it is this faculty, which, though by slow degrees, draws them out of their original condition, in which his days would slide away insensibly in peace and innocence; that it is this faculty, which, in a succession of ages, produces his discoveries and mistakes, his virtues and his vices, and, at long run, renders him both his own and nature's tyrant. It would be shocking to be obliged to commend, as a beneficent being, whoever he was that first suggested to the Oronoco Indians the use of those boards which they bind on the temples of their children, and which secure to them the enjoyment of some part at least of their natural imbecility and happiness.

Savage man, abandoned by nature to pure instinct, or rather indemnified for that which has perhaps been denied to him by faculties capable of immediately supplying the place of it, and of raising him afterwards a great deal higher, would therefore begin with functions that were merely animal: to see and to feel would be his first condition, which he would enjoy in common with other animals. To will and not to will, to wish and to fear, would be the first, and in a manner, the only operations of his soul, till new circumstances occasioned new developments.

Let moralists say what they will, the human understanding is greatly indebted to the passions, which, on their side, are likewise universally allowed to be greatly indebted to the human understanding. It is by the activity of our passions, that our reason improves: we covet knowledge merely because we covet enjoyment, and it is impossible to conceive why a man exempt from fears and desires should take the trouble to reason. The passions, in their turn, owe their origin to our wants, and their increase to our progress in science; for we cannot desire or fear anything, but in consequence of the ideas we have of it, or of the simple impulses of nature; and savage man, destitute of every species of knowledge, experiences no passions but those of this last kind; his desires never extend beyond his physical wants; he knows no goods but food, a female, and rest; he fears no evil but pain, and hunger; I say pain, and not death; for no animal, merely as such, will ever know what it is to die, and the knowledge of death, and of its terrors, is one of the first acquisitions made by man, in consequence of his deviating from the animal state.

I could easily, were it requisite, cite facts in support of this opinion, and show, that the progress of the mind has everywhere kept pace exactly with the wants, to which nature had left the inhabitants exposed, or to which circumstances had subjected them, and consequently to the passions, which inclined them to provide for these wants. I could exhibit in Egypt the arts starting up, and extending themselves with the inundations of the Nile; I could pursue them in their progress among the Greeks, where they were seen to bud forth, grow, and rise to the heavens, in the midst of the sands and rocks of Attica, without being able to take root on the fertile banks of the Eurotas; I would observe that, in general, the inhabitants of the north are more industrious than those of the south, because they can less do without industry; as if nature thus meant to make all things equal, by giving to the mind that fertility she has denied to the soil.

But exclusive of the uncertain testimonies of history, who does not perceive that everything seems to remove from savage man the temptation and the means of altering his condition? His imagination paints nothing to him; his heart asks nothing from him. His moderate wants are so easily supplied with what he everywhere finds ready to his hand, and he stands at such a distance from the degree of knowledge requisite to covet more, that he can neither have foresight nor curiosity. The spectacle of nature, by growing quite familiar to him, becomes at last equally indifferent. It is constantly the same order, constantly the same revolutions; he has not sense enough to feel surprise at the sight of the greatest wonders; and it is not in his mind we must look for that philosophy, which man must have to know how to observe once, what he has every day seen. His soul, which nothing disturbs, gives itself up entirely to the consciousness of its actual existence, without any thought of even the nearest futurity; and his projects, equally confined with his views, scarce extend to the end of the day. Such is, even at present, the degree of foresight in the Caribbean: he sells his cotton bed in the morning, and comes in the evening, with tears in his eyes, to buy it back, not having foreseen that he should want it again the next night.

The more we meditate on this subject, the wider does the distance between mere sensation and the most simple knowledge become in our eyes; and it is impossible to conceive how man, by his own powers alone, without the assistance of communication, and the spur of necessity, could have got over so great an interval. How many ages perhaps revolved, before men beheld any other fire but that of the heavens? How many different accidents must have concurred to make them acquainted with the most common uses of this element? How often have they let it go out, before they knew the art of reproducing it? And how often perhaps has not every one of these secrets perished with the discoverer? What shall we say of agriculture, an art which requires so much labour and foresight; which depends upon other arts; which, it is very evident, cannot be practised but in a society, if not a formed one, at least one of some standing, and which does not so much serve to draw aliments from the earth, for the earth would yield them without all that trouble, as to oblige her to produce those things, which we like best, preferably to others? But let us suppose that men had multiplied to such a degree, that the natural products of the earth no longer sufficed for their support; a supposition which, by the bye, would prove that this kind of life would be very advantageous to the human species; let us suppose that, without forge or anvil, the instruments of husbandry had dropped from the heavens into the hands of savages, that these men had got the better of that mortal aversion they all have for constant labour; that they had learned to foretell their wants at so great a distance of time; that they had guessed exactly how they were to break the earth, commit their seed to it, and plant trees; that they had found out the art of grinding their corn, and improving by fermentation the juice of their grapes; all operations which we must allow them to have learned from the gods, since we cannot conceive how they should make such discoveries of themselves; after all these fine presents, what man would be mad enough to cultivate a field, that may be robbed by the first comer, man or beast, who takes a fancy to the produce of it. And would any man consent to spend his day in labour and fatigue, when the rewards of his labour and fatigue became more and more precarious in proportion to his want of them? In a word, how could this situation engage men to cultivate the earth, as long as it was not parcelled out among them, that is, as long as a state of nature subsisted.

Though we should suppose savage man as well versed in the art of thinking, as philosophers make him; though we were, after them, to make him a philosopher himself, discovering of himself the sublimest truths, forming to himself, by the most abstract arguments, maxims of justice and reason drawn from the love of order in general, or from the known will of his Creator: in a word, though we were to suppose his mind as intelligent and enlightened, as it must, and is, in fact, found to be dull and stupid; what benefit would the species receive from all these metaphysical discoveries, which could not be communicated, but must perish with the individual who had made them? What progress could mankind make in the forests, scattered up and down among the other animals? And to what degree could men mutually improve and enlighten each other, when they had no fixed habitation, nor any need of each other's assistance; when the same persons scarcely met twice in their whole lives, and on meeting neither spoke to, or so much as knew each other?

Let us consider how many ideas we owe to the use of speech; how much grammar exercises, and facilitates the operations of the mind; let us, besides, reflect on the immense pains and time that the first invention of languages must have required: Let us add these reflections to the preceding; and then we may judge how many thousand ages must have been requisite to develop successively the operations, which the human mind is capable of producing.

I must now beg leave to stop one moment to consider the perplexities attending the origin of languages. I might here barely cite or repeat the researches made, in relation to this question, by the Abbe de Condillac, which all fully confirm my system, and perhaps even suggested to me the first idea of it. But, as the manner, in which the philosopher resolves the difficulties of his own starting, concerning the origin of arbitrary signs, shows that he supposes, what I doubt, namely a kind of society already established among the inventors of languages; I think it my duty, at the same time that I refer to his reflections, to give my own, in order to expose the same difficulties in a light suitable to my subject. The first that offers is how languages could become necessary; for as there was no correspondence between men, nor the least necessity for any, there is no conceiving the necessity of this invention, nor the possibility of it, if it was not indispensable. I might say, with many others, that languages are the fruit of the domestic intercourse between fathers, mothers, and children: but this, besides its not answering any difficulties, would be committing the same fault with those, who reasoning on the state of nature, transfer to it ideas collected in society, always consider families as living together under one roof, and their members as observing among themselves an union, equally intimate and permanent with that which we see exist in a civil state, where so many common interests conspire to unite them; whereas in this primitive state, as there were neither houses nor cabins, nor any kind of property, every one took up his lodging at random, and seldom continued above one night in the same place; males and females united without any premeditated design, as chance, occasion, or desire brought them together, nor had they any great occasion for language to make known their thoughts to each other. They parted with the same ease. The mother suckled her children, when just born, for her own sake; but afterwards out of love and affection to them, when habit and custom had made them dear to her; but they no sooner gained strength enough to run about in quest of food than they separated even from her of their own accord; and as they scarce had any other method of not losing each other, than that of remaining constantly in each other's sight, they soon came to such a pass of forgetfulness, as not even to know each other, when they happened to meet again. I must further observe that the child having all his wants to explain, and consequently more things to say to his mother, than the mother can have to say to him, it is he that must be at the chief expense of invention, and the language he makes use of must be in a great measure his own work; this makes the number of languages equal to that of the individuals who are to speak them; and this multiplicity of languages is further increased by their roving and vagabond kind of life, which allows no idiom time enough to acquire any consistency; for to say that the mother would have dictated to the child the words he must employ to ask her this thing and that, may well enough explain in what manner languages, already formed, are taught, but it does not show us in what manner they are first formed.

Let us suppose this first difficulty conquered: Let us for a moment consider ourselves at this side of the immense space, which must have separated the pure state of nature from that in which languages became necessary, and let us, after allowing such necessity, examine how languages could begin to be established. A new difficulty this, still more stubborn than the preceding; for if men stood in need of speech to learn to think, they must have stood in still greater need of the art of thinking to invent that of speaking; and though we could conceive how the sounds of the voice came to be taken for the conventional interpreters of our ideas we should not be the nearer knowing who could have been the interpreters of this convention for such ideas, as, in consequence of their not having any sensible objects, could not be made manifest by gesture or voice; so that we can scarce form any tolerable conjectures concerning the birth of this art of communicating our thoughts, and establishing a correspondence between minds: a sublime art which, though so remote from its origin, philosophers still behold at such a prodigious distance from its perfection, that I never met with one of them bold enough to affirm it would ever arrive there, though the revolutions necessarily produced by time were suspended in its favour; though prejudice could be banished from, or would be at least content to sit silent in the presence of our academies, and though these societies should consecrate themselves, entirely and during whole ages, to the study of this intricate object.

The first language of man, the most universal and most energetic of all languages, in short, the only language he had occasion for, before there was a necessity of persuading assembled multitudes, was the cry of nature. As this cry was never extorted but by a kind of instinct in the most urgent cases, to implore assistance in great danger, or relief in great sufferings, it was of little use in the common occurrences of life, where more moderate sentiments generally prevail. When the ideas of men began to extend and multiply, and a closer communication began to take place among them, they laboured to devise more numerous signs, and a more extensive language: they multiplied the inflections of the voice, and added to them gestures, which are, in their own nature, more expressive, and whose meaning depends less on any prior determination. They therefore expressed visible and movable objects by gestures and those which strike the ear, by imitative sounds: but as gestures scarcely indicate anything except objects that are actually present or can be easily described, and visible actions; as they are not of general use, since darkness or the interposition of an opaque medium renders them useless; and as besides they require attention rather than excite it: men at length bethought themselves of substituting for them the articulations of voice, which, without having the same relation to any determinate object, are, in quality of instituted signs, fitter to represent all our ideas; a substitution, which could only have been made by common consent, and in a manner pretty difficult to practise by men, whose rude organs were unimproved by exercise; a substitution, which is in itself more difficult to be conceived, since the motives to this unanimous agreement must have been somehow or another expressed, and speech therefore appears to have been exceedingly requisite to establish the use of speech.

We must allow that the words, first made use of by men, had in their minds a much more extensive signification, than those employed in languages of some standing, and that, considering how ignorant they were of the division of speech into its constituent parts; they at first gave every word the meaning of an entire proposition. When afterwards they began to perceive the difference between the subject and attribute, and between verb and noun, a distinction which required no mean effort of genius, the substantives for a time were only so many proper names, the infinitive was the only tense, and as to adjectives, great difficulties must have attended the development of the idea that represents them, since every adjective is an abstract word, and abstraction is an unnatural and very painful operation.

At first they gave every object a peculiar name, without any regard to its genus or species, things which these first institutors of language were in no condition to distinguish; and every individual presented itself solitary to their minds, as it stands in the table of nature. If they called one oak A, they called another oak B: so that their dictionary must have been more extensive in proportion as their knowledge of things was more confined. It could not but be a very difficult task to get rid of so diffuse and embarrassing a nomenclature; as in order to marshal the several beings under common and generic denominations, it was necessary to be first acquainted with their properties, and their differences; to be stocked with observations and definitions, that is to say, to understand natural history and metaphysics, advantages which the men of these times could not have enjoyed.

Besides, general ideas cannot be conveyed to the mind without the assistance of words, nor can the understanding seize them without the assistance of propositions. This is one of the reasons, why mere animals cannot form such ideas, nor ever acquire the perfectibility which depends on such an operation. When a monkey leaves without the least hesitation one nut for another, are we to think he has any general idea of that kind of fruit, and that he compares these two individual bodies with his archetype notion of them? No, certainly; but the sight of one of these nuts calls back to his memory the sensations which he has received from the other; and his eyes, modified after some certain manner, give notice to his palate of the modification it is in its turn going to receive. Every general idea is purely intellectual; let the imagination tamper ever so little with it, it immediately becomes a particular idea. Endeavour to represent to yourself the image of a tree in general, you never will be able to do it; in spite of all your efforts it will appear big or little, thin or tufted, of a bright or a deep colour; and were you master to see nothing in it, but what can be seen in every tree, such a picture would no longer resemble any tree. Beings perfectly abstract are perceivable in the same manner, or are only conceivable by the assistance of speech. The definition of a triangle can alone give you a just idea of that figure: the moment you form a triangle in your mind, it is this or that particular triangle and no other, and you cannot avoid giving breadth to its lines and colour to its area. We must therefore make use of propositions; we must therefore speak to have general ideas; for the moment the imagination stops, the mind must stop too, if not assisted by speech. If therefore the first inventors could give no names to any ideas but those they had already, it follows that the first substantives could never have been anything more than proper names.

But when by means, which I cannot conceive, our new grammarians began to extend their ideas, and generalize their words, the ignorance of the inventors must have confined this method to very narrow bounds; and as they had at first too much multiplied the names of individuals for want of being acquainted with the distinctions called genus and species, they afterwards made too few genera and species for want of having considered beings in all their differences; to push the divisions far enough, they must have had more knowledge and experience than we can allow them, and have made more researches and taken more pains, than we can suppose them willing to submit to. Now if, even at this present time, we every day discover new species, which had before escaped all our observations, how many species must have escaped the notice of men, who judged of things merely from their first appearances! As to the primitive classes and the most general notions, it were superfluous to add that these they must have likewise overlooked: how, for example, could they have thought of or understood the words, matter, spirit, substance, mode, figure, motion, since even our philosophers, who for so long a time have been constantly employing these terms, can themselves scarcely understand them, and since the ideas annexed to these words being purely metaphysical, no models of them could be found in nature?

I stop at these first advances, and beseech my judges to suspend their lecture a little, in order to consider, what a great way language has still to go, in regard to the invention of physical substantives alone, (though the easiest part of language to invent,) to be able to express all the sentiments of man, to assume an invariable form, to bear being spoken in public and to influence society: I earnestly entreat them to consider how much time and knowledge must have been requisite to find out numbers, abstract words, the aorists, and all the other tenses of verbs, the particles, and syntax, the method of connecting propositions and arguments, of forming all the logic of discourse. For my own part, I am so scared at the difficulties that multiply at every step, and so convinced of the almost demonstrated impossibility of languages owing their birth and establishment to means that were merely human, that I must leave to whoever may please to take it up, the task of discussing this difficult problem. "Which was the most necessary, society already formed to invent languages, or languages already invented to form society?"

But be the case of these origins ever so mysterious, we may at least infer from the little care which nature has taken to bring men together by mutual wants, and make the use of speech easy to them, how little she has done towards making them sociable, and how little she has contributed to anything which they themselves have done to become so. In fact, it is impossible to conceive, why, in this primitive state, one man should have more occasion for the assistance of another, than one monkey, or one wolf for that of another animal of the same species; or supposing that he had, what motive could induce another to assist him; or even, in this last case, how he, who wanted assistance, and he from whom it was wanted, could agree among themselves upon the conditions. Authors, I know, are continually telling us, that in this state man would have been a most miserable creature; and if it is true, as I fancy I have proved it, that he must have continued many ages without either the desire or the opportunity of emerging from such a state, this their assertion could only serve to justify a charge against nature, and not any against the being which nature had thus constituted; but, if I thoroughly understand this term miserable, it is a word, that either has no meaning, or signifies nothing, but a privation attended with pain, and a suffering state of body or soul; now I would fain know what kind of misery can be that of a free being, whose heart enjoys perfect peace, and body perfect health? And which is aptest to become insupportable to those who enjoy it, a civil or a natural life? In civil life we can scarcely meet a single person who does not complain of his existence; many even throw away as much of it as they can, and the united force of divine and human laws can hardly put bounds to this disorder. Was ever any free savage known to have been so much as tempted to complain of life, and lay violent hands on himself? Let us therefore judge with less pride on which side real misery is to be placed. Nothing, on the contrary, must have been so unhappy as savage man, dazzled by flashes of knowledge, racked by passions, and reasoning on a state different from that in which he saw himself placed. It was in consequence of a very wise Providence, that the faculties, which he potentially enjoyed, were not to develop themselves but in proportion as there offered occasions to exercise them, lest they should be superfluous or troublesome to him when he did not want them, or tardy and useless when he did. He had in his instinct alone everything requisite to live in a state of nature; in his cultivated reason he has barely what is necessary to live in a state of society.

It appears at first sight that, as there was no kind of moral relations between men in this state, nor any known duties, they could not be either good or bad, and had neither vices nor virtues, unless we take these words in a physical sense, and call vices, in the individual, the qualities which may prove detrimental to his own preservation, and virtues those which may contribute to it; in which case we should be obliged to consider him as most virtuous, who made least resistance against the simple impulses of nature. But without deviating from the usual meaning of these terms, it is proper to suspend the judgment we might form of such a situation, and be upon our guard against prejudice, till, the balance in hand, we have examined whether there are more virtues or vices among civilized men; or whether the improvement of their understanding is sufficient to compensate the damage which they mutually do to each other, in proportion as they become better informed of the services which they ought to do; or whether, upon the whole, they would not be much happier in a condition, where they had nothing to fear or to hope from each other, than in that where they had submitted to an universal subserviency, and have obliged themselves to depend for everything upon the good will of those, who do not think themselves obliged to give anything in return.

But above all things let us beware concluding with Hobbes, that man, as having no idea of goodness, must be naturally bad; that he is vicious because he does not know what virtue is; that he always refuses to do any service to those of his own species, because he believes that none is due to them; that, in virtue of that right which he justly claims to everything he wants, he foolishly looks upon himself as proprietor of the whole universe. Hobbes very plainly saw the flaws in all the modern definitions of natural right: but the consequences, which he draws from his own definition, show that it is, in the sense he understands it, equally exceptionable. This author, to argue from his own principles, should say that the state of nature, being that where the care of our own preservation interferes least with the preservation of others, was of course the most favourable to peace, and most suitable to mankind; whereas he advances the very reverse in consequence of his having injudiciously admitted, as objects of that care which savage man should take of his preservation, the satisfaction of numberless passions which are the work of society, and have rendered laws necessary. A bad man, says he, is a robust child. But this is not proving that savage man is a robust child; and though we were to grant that he was, what could this philosopher infer from such a concession? That if this man, when robust, depended on others as much as when feeble, there is no excess that he would not be guilty of. He would make nothing of striking his mother when she delayed ever so little to give him the breast; he would claw, and bite, and strangle without remorse the first of his younger brothers, that ever so accidentally jostled or otherwise disturbed him. But these are two contradictory suppositions in the state of nature, to be robust and dependent. Man is weak when dependent, and his own master before he grows robust. Hobbes did not consider that the same cause, which hinders savages from making use of their reason, as our jurisconsults pretend, hinders them at the same time from making an ill use of their faculties, as he himself pretends; so that we may say that savages are not bad, precisely because they don't know what it is to be good; for it is neither the development of the understanding, nor the curb of the law, but the calmness of their passions and their ignorance of vice that hinders them from doing ill: _tantus plus in illis proficit vitiorum ignorantia, quam in his cognito virtutis_. There is besides another principle that has escaped Hobbes, and which, having been given to man to moderate, on certain occasions, the blind and impetuous sallies of self-love, or the desire of self-preservation previous to the appearance of that passion, allays the ardour, with which he naturally pursues his private welfare, by an innate abhorrence to see beings suffer that resemble him. I shall not surely be contradicted, in granting to man the only natural virtue, which the most passionate detractor of human virtues could not deny him, I mean that of pity, a disposition suitable to creatures weak as we are, and liable to so many evils; a virtue so much the more universal, and withal useful to man, as it takes place in him of all manner of reflection; and so natural, that the beasts themselves sometimes give evident signs of it. Not to speak of the tenderness of mothers for their young; and of the dangers they face to screen them from danger; with what reluctance are horses known to trample upon living bodies; one animal never passes unmoved by the dead carcass of another animal of the same species: there are even some who bestow a kind of sepulture upon their dead fellows;

and the mournful lowings of cattle, on their entering the slaughter-house, publish the impression made upon them by the horrible spectacle they are there struck with. It is with pleasure we see the author of the fable of the bees, forced to acknowledge man a compassionate and sensible being; and lay aside, in the example he offers to confirm it, his cold and subtle style, to place before us the pathetic picture of a man, who, with his hands tied up, is obliged to behold a beast of prey tear a child from the arms of his mother, and then with his teeth grind the tender limbs, and with his claws rend the throbbing entrails of the innocent victim. What horrible emotions must not such a spectator experience at the sight of an event which does not personally concern him? What anguish must he not suffer at his not being able to assist the fainting mother or the expiring infant?

Such is the pure motion of nature, anterior to all manner of reflection; such is the force of natural pity, which the most dissolute manners have as yet found it so difficult to extinguish, since we every day see, in our theatrical representation, those men sympathize with the unfortunate and weep at their sufferings, who, if in the tyrant's place, would aggravate the torments of their enemies. Mandeville was very sensible that men, in spite of all their morality, would never have been better than monsters, if nature had not given them pity to assist reason: but he did not perceive that from this quality alone flow all the social virtues, which he would dispute mankind the possession of. In fact, what is generosity, what clemency, what humanity, but pity applied to the weak, to the guilty, or to the human species in general? Even benevolence and friendship, if we judge right, will appear the effects of a constant pity, fixed upon a particular object: for to wish that a person may not suffer, what is it but to wish that he may be happy? Though it were true that commiseration is no more than a sentiment, which puts us in the place of him who suffers, a sentiment obscure but active in the savage, developed but dormant in civilized man, how could this notion affect the truth of what I advance, but to make it more evident. In fact, commiseration must be so much the more energetic, the more intimately the animal, that beholds any kind of distress, identifies himself with the animal that labours under it. Now it is evident that this identification must have been infinitely more perfect in the state of nature than in the state of reason. It is reason that engenders self-love, and reflection that strengthens it; it is reason that makes man shrink into himself; it is reason that makes him keep aloof from everything that can trouble or afflict him: it is philosophy that destroys his connections with other men; it is in consequence of her dictates that he mutters to himself at the sight of another in distress, You may perish for aught I care, nothing can hurt me. Nothing less than those evils, which threaten the whole species, can disturb the calm sleep of the philosopher, and force him from his bed. One man may with impunity murder another under his windows; he has nothing to do but clap his hands to his ears, argue a little with himself to hinder nature, that startles within him, from identifying him with the unhappy sufferer. Savage man wants this admirable talent; and for want of wisdom and reason, is always ready foolishly to obey the first whispers of humanity. In riots and street-brawls the populace flock together, the prudent man sneaks off. They are the dregs of the people, the poor basket and barrow-women, that part the combatants, and hinder gentle folks from cutting one another's throats.

It is therefore certain that pity is a natural sentiment, which, by moderating in every individual the activity of self-love, contributes to the mutual preservation of the whole species. It is this pity which hurries us without reflection to the assistance of those we see in distress; it is this pity which, in a state of nature, stands for laws, for manners, for virtue, with this advantage, that no one is tempted to disobey her sweet and gentle voice: it is this pity which will always hinder a robust savage from plundering a feeble child, or infirm old man, of the subsistence they have acquired with pain and difficulty, if he has but the least prospect of providing for himself by any other means: it is this pity which, instead of that sublime maxim of argumentative justice, Do to others as you would have others do to you, inspires all men with that other maxim of natural goodness a great deal less perfect, but perhaps more useful, Consult your own happiness with as little prejudice as you can to that of others. It is in a word, in this natural sentiment, rather than in fine-spun arguments, that we must look for the cause of that reluctance which every man would experience to do evil, even independently of the maxims of education. Though it may be the peculiar happiness of Socrates and other geniuses of his stamp, to reason themselves into virtue, the human species would long ago have ceased to exist, had it depended entirely for its preservation on the reasonings of the individuals that compose it.

With passions so tame, and so salutary a curb, men, rather wild than wicked, and more attentive to guard against mischief than to do any to other animals, were not exposed to any dangerous dissensions: As they kept up no manner of correspondence with each other, and were of course strangers to vanity, to respect, to esteem, to contempt; as they had no notion of what we call Meum and Tuum, nor any true idea of justice; as they considered any violence they were liable to, as an evil that could be easily repaired, and not as an injury that deserved punishment; and as they never so much as dreamed of revenge, unless perhaps mechanically and unpremeditatedly, as a dog who bites the stone that has been thrown at him; their disputes could seldom be attended with bloodshed, were they never occasioned by a more considerable stake than that of subsistence: but there is a more dangerous subject of contention, which I must not leave unnoticed.

Among the passions which ruffle the heart of man, there is one of a hot and impetuous nature, which renders the sexes necessary to each other; a terrible passion which despises all dangers, bears down all obstacles, and to which in its transports it seems proper to destroy the human species which it is destined to preserve. What must become of men abandoned to this lawless and brutal rage, without modesty, without shame, and every day disputing the objects of their passion at the expense of their blood?

We must in the first place allow that the more violent the passions, the more necessary are laws to restrain them: but besides that the disorders and the crimes, to which these passions daily give rise among us, sufficiently grove the insufficiency of laws for that purpose, we would do well to look back a little further and examine, if these evils did not spring up with the laws themselves; for at this rate, though the laws were capable of repressing these evils, it is the least that might be expected from them, seeing it is no more than stopping the progress of a mischief which they themselves have produced.

Let us begin by distinguishing between what is moral and what is physical in the passion called love. The physical part of it is that general desire which prompts the sexes to unite with each other; the moral part is that which determines that desire, and fixes it upon a particular object to the exclusion of all others, or at least gives it a greater degree of energy for this preferred object. Now it is easy to perceive that the moral part of love is a factitious sentiment, engendered by society, and cried up by the women with great care and address in order to establish their empire, and secure command to that sex which ought to obey. This sentiment, being founded on certain notions of beauty and merit which a savage is not capable of having, and upon comparisons which he is not capable of making, can scarcely exist in him: for as his mind was never in a condition to form abstract ideas of regularity and proportion, neither is his heart susceptible of sentiments of admiration and love, which, even without our perceiving it, are produced by our application of these ideas; he listens solely to the dispositions implanted in him by nature, and not to taste which he never was in a way of acquiring; and every woman answers his purpose.

Confined entirely to what is physical in love, and happy enough not to know these preferences which sharpen the appetite for it, at the same time that they increase the difficulty of satisfying such appetite, men, in a state of nature, must be subject to fewer and less violent fits of that passion, and of course there must be fewer and less violent disputes among them in consequence of it. The imagination which causes so many ravages among us, never speaks to the heart of savages, who peaceably wait for the impulses of nature, yield to these impulses without choice and with more pleasure than fury; and whose desires never outlive their necessity for the thing desired.

Nothing therefore can be more evident, than that it is society alone, which has added even to love itself as well as to all the other passions, that impetuous ardour, which so often renders it fatal to mankind; and it is so much the more ridiculous to represent savages constantly murdering each other to glut their brutality, as this opinion is diametrically opposite to experience, and the Caribbeans, the people in the world who have as yet deviated least from the state of nature, are to all intents and purposes the most peaceable in their amours, and the least subject to jealousy, though they live in a burning climate which seems always to add considerably to the activity of these passions.

As to the inductions which may be drawn, in respect to several species of animals, from the battles of the males, who in all seasons cover our poultry yards with blood, and in spring particularly cause our forests to ring again with the noise they make in disputing their females, we must begin by excluding all those species, where nature has evidently established, in the relative power of the sexes, relations different from those which exist among us: thus from the battle of cocks we can form no induction that will affect the human species. In the species, where the proportion is better observed, these battles must be owing entirely to the fewness of the females compared with the males, or, which is all one, to the exclusive intervals, during which the females constantly refuse the addresses of the males; for if the female admits the male but two months in the year, it is all the same as if the number of females were five-sixths less than what it is: now neither of these cases is applicable to the human species, where the number of females generally surpasses that of males, and where it has never been observed that, even among savages, the females had, like those of other animals, stated times of passion and indifference, Besides, among several of these animals the whole species takes fire all at once, and for some days nothing is, to be seen among them but confusion, tumult, disorder and bloodshed; a state unknown to the human species where love is never periodical. We can not therefore conclude from the battles of certain animals for the possession of their females, that the same would be the case of man in a state of nature; and though we might, as these contests do not destroy the other species, there is at least equal room to think they would not be fatal to ours; nay it is very probable that they would cause fewer ravages than they do in society, especially in those countries where, morality being as yet held in some esteem, the jealousy of lovers, and the vengeance of husbands every day produce duels, murders and even worse crimes; where the duty of an eternal fidelity serves only to propagate adultery; and the very laws of continence and honour necessarily contribute to increase dissoluteness, and multiply abortions.

Let us conclude that savage man, wandering about in the forests, without industry, without speech, without any fixed residence, an equal stranger to war and every social connection, without standing in any shape in need of his fellows, as well as without any desire of hurting them, and perhaps even without ever distinguishing them individually one from the other, subject to few passions, and finding in himself all he wants, let us, I say, conclude that savage man thus circumstanced had no knowledge or sentiment but such as are proper to that condition, that he was alone sensible of his real necessities, took notice of nothing but what it was his interest to see, and that his understanding made as little progress as his vanity. If he happened to make any discovery, he could the less communicate it as he did not even know his children. The art perished with the inventor; there was neither education nor improvement; generations succeeded generations to no purpose; and as all constantly set out from the same point, whole centuries rolled on in the rudeness and barbarity of the first age; the species was grown old, while the individual still remained in a state of childhood.

If I have enlarged so much upon the supposition of this primitive condition, it is because I thought it my duty, considering what ancient errors and inveterate prejudices I have to extirpate, to dig to the very roots, and show in a true picture of the state of nature, how much even natural inequality falls short in this state of that reality and influence which our writers ascribe to it.

In fact, we may easily perceive that among the differences, which distinguish men, several pass for natural, which are merely the work of habit and the different kinds of life adopted by men living in a social way. Thus a robust or delicate constitution, and the strength and weakness which depend on it, are oftener produced by the hardy or effeminate manner in which a man has been brought up, than by the primitive constitution of his body. It is the same thus in regard to the forces of the mind; and education not only produces a difference between those minds which are cultivated and those which are not, but even increases that which is found among the first in proportion to their culture; for let a giant and a dwarf set out in the same path, the giant at every step will acquire a new advantage over the dwarf. Now, if we compare the prodigious variety in the education and manner of living of the different orders of men in a civil state, with the simplicity and uniformity that prevails in the animal and savage life, where all the individuals make use of the same aliments, live in the same manner, and do exactly the same things, we shall easily conceive how much the difference between man and man in the state of nature must be less than in the state of society, and how much every inequality of institution must increase the natural inequalities of the human species.

But though nature in the distribution of her gifts should really affect all the preferences that are ascribed to her, what advantage could the most favoured derive from her partiality, to the prejudice of others, in a state of things, which scarce admitted any kind of relation between her pupils? Of what service can beauty be, where there is no love? What will wit avail people who don't speak, or craft those who have no affairs to transact? Authors are constantly crying out, that the strongest would oppress the weakest; but let them explain what they mean by the word oppression. One man will rule with violence, another will groan under a constant subjection to all his caprices: this is indeed precisely what I observe among us, but I don't see how it can be said of savage men, into whose heads it would be a harder matter to drive even the meaning of the words domination and servitude. One man might, indeed, seize on the fruits which another had gathered, on the game which another had killed, on the cavern which another had occupied for shelter; but how is it possible he should ever exact obedience from him, and what chains of dependence can there be among men who possess nothing? If I am driven from one tree, I have nothing to do but look out for another; if one place is made uneasy to me, what can hinder me from taking up my quarters elsewhere? But suppose I should meet a man so much superior to me in strength, and withal so wicked, so lazy and so barbarous as to oblige me to provide for his subsistence while he remains idle; he must resolve not to take his eyes from me a single moment, to bind me fast before he can take the least nap, lest I should kill him or give him the slip during his sleep: that is to say, he must expose himself voluntarily to much greater troubles than what he seeks to avoid, than any he gives me. And after all, let him abate ever so little of his vigilance; let him at some sudden noise but turn his head another way; I am already buried in the forest, my fetters are broke, and he never sees me again.

But without insisting any longer upon these details, every one must see that, as the bonds of servitude are formed merely by the mutual dependence of men one upon another and the reciprocal necessities which unite them, it is impossible for one man to enslave another, without having first reduced him to a condition in which he can not live without the enslaver's assistance; a condition which, as it does not exist in a state of nature, must leave every man his own master, and render the law of the strongest altogether vain and useless.

Having proved that the inequality, which may subsist between man and man in a state of nature, is almost imperceivable, and that it has very little influence, I must now proceed to show its origin, and trace its progress, in the successive developments of the human mind. After having showed, that perfectibility, the social virtues, and the other faculties, which natural man had received _in potentia_, could never be developed of themselves, that for that purpose there was a necessity for the fortuitous concurrence of several foreign causes, which might never happen, and without which he must have eternally remained in his primitive condition; I must proceed to consider and bring together the different accidents which may have perfected the human understanding by debasing the species, render a being wicked by rendering him sociable, and from so remote a term bring man at last and the world to the point in which we now see them.

I must own that, as the events I am about to describe might have happened many different ways, my choice of these I shall assign can be grounded on nothing but mere conjecture; but besides these conjectures becoming reasons, when they are not only the most probable that can be drawn from the nature of things, but the only means we can have of discovering truth, the consequences I mean to deduce from mine will not be merely conjectural, since, on the principles I have just established, it is impossible to form any other system, that would not supply me with the same results, and from which I might not draw the same conclusions.

This will authorize me to be the more concise in my reflections on the manner, in which the lapse of time makes amends for the little verisimilitude of events; on the surprising power of very trivial causes, when they act without intermission; on the impossibility there is on the one hand of destroying certain Hypotheses, if on the other we can not give them the degree of certainty which facts must be allowed to possess; on its being the business of history, when two facts are proposed, as real, to be connected by a chain of intermediate facts which are either unknown or considered as such, to furnish such facts as may actually connect them; and the business of philosophy, when history is silent, to point out similar facts which may answer the same purpose; in fine on the privilege of similitude, in regard to events, to reduce facts to a much smaller number of different classes than is generally imagined. It suffices me to offer these objects to the consideration of my judges; it suffices me to have conducted my inquiry in such a manner as to save common readers the trouble of considering them.

SECOND PART

The first man, who, after enclosing a piece of ground, took it into his head to say, "This is mine," and found people simple enough to believe him, was the true founder of civil society. How many crimes, how many wars, how many murders, how many misfortunes and horrors, would that man have saved the human species, who pulling up the stakes or filling up the ditches should have cried to his fellows: Be sure not to listen to this imposter; you are lost, if you forget that the fruits of the earth belong equally to us all, and the earth itself to nobody! But it is highly probable that things were now come to such a pass, that they could not continue much longer in the same way; for as this idea of property depends on several prior ideas which could only spring up gradually one after another, it was not formed all at once in the human mind: men must have made great progress; they must have acquired a great stock of industry and knowledge, and transmitted and increased it from age to age before they could arrive at this last term of the state of nature. Let us therefore take up things a little higher, and collect into one point of view, and in their most natural order, this slow succession of events and mental improvements.

The first sentiment of man was that of his existence, his first care that of preserving it. The productions of the earth yielded him all the assistance he required; instinct prompted him to make use of them. Among the various appetites, which made him at different times experience different modes of existence, there was one that excited him to perpetuate his species; and this blind propensity, quite void of anything like pure love or affection, produced nothing but an act that was merely animal. The present heat once allayed, the sexes took no further notice of each other, and even the child ceased to have any tie in his mother, the moment he ceased to want her assistance.

Such was the condition of infant man; such was the life of an animal confined at first to pure sensations, and so far from harbouring any thought of forcing her gifts from nature, that he scarcely availed himself of those which she offered to him of her own accord. But difficulties soon arose, and there was a necessity for learning how to surmount them: the height of some trees, which prevented his reaching their fruits; the competition of other animals equally fond of the same fruits; the fierceness of many that even aimed at his life; these were so many circumstances, which obliged him to apply to bodily exercise. There was a necessity for becoming active, swift-footed, and sturdy in battle. The natural arms, which are stones and the branches of trees, soon offered themselves to his assistance. He learned to surmount the obstacles of nature, to contend in case of necessity with other animals, to dispute his subsistence even with other men, or indemnify himself for the loss of whatever he found himself obliged to part with to the strongest.

In proportion as the human species grew more numerous, and extended itself, its pains likewise multiplied and increased. The difference of soils, climates and seasons, might have forced men to observe some difference in their way of living. Bad harvests, long and severe winters, and scorching summers which parched up all the fruits of the earth, required extraordinary exertions of industry. On the sea shore, and the banks of rivers, they invented the line and the hook, and became fishermen and ichthyophagous. In the forests they made themselves bows and arrows, and became huntsmen and warriors. In the cold countries they covered themselves with the skins of the beasts they had killed; thunder, a volcano, or some happy accident made them acquainted with fire, a new resource against the rigours of winter: they discovered the method of preserving this element, then that of reproducing it, and lastly the way of preparing with it the flesh of animals, which heretofore they devoured raw from the carcass.

This reiterated application of various beings to himself, and to one another, must have naturally engendered in the mind of man the idea of certain relations. These relations, which we express by the words, great, little, strong, weak, swift, slow, fearful, bold, and the like, compared occasionally, and almost without thinking of it, produced in him some kind of reflection, or rather a mechanical prudence, which pointed out to him the precautions most essential to his preservation and safety.

The new lights resulting from this development increased his superiority over other animals, by making him sensible of it. He laid himself out to ensnare them; he played them a thousand tricks; and though several surpassed him in strength or in swiftness, he in time became the master of those that could be of any service to him, and a sore enemy to those that could do him any mischief. 'Tis thus, that the first look he gave into himself produced the first emotion of pride in him; 'tis thus that, at a time he scarce knew how to distinguish between the different ranks of existence, by attributing to his species the first rank among animals in general, he prepared himself at a distance to pretend to it as an individual among those of his own species in particular.

Though other men were not to him what they are to us, and he had scarce more intercourse with them than with other animals, they were not overlooked in his observations. The conformities, which in time he might discover between them, and between himself and his female, made him judge of those he did not perceive; and seeing that they all behaved as himself would have done in similar circumstances, he concluded that their manner of thinking and willing was quite conformable to his own; and this important truth, when once engraved deeply on his mind, made him follow, by a presentiment as sure as any logic, and withal much quicker, the best rules of conduct, which for the sake of his own safety and advantage it was proper he should observe towards them.

Instructed by experience that the love of happiness is the sole principle of all human actions, he found himself in a condition to distinguish the few cases, in which common interest might authorize him to build upon the assistance of his fellows, and those still fewer, in which a competition of interests might justly render it suspected. In the first case he united with them in the same flock, or at most by some kind of free association which obliged none of its members, and lasted no longer than the transitory necessity that had given birth to it. In the second case every one aimed at his own private advantage, either by open force if he found himself strong enough, or by cunning and address if he thought himself too weak to use violence.

Such was the manner in which men might have insensibly acquired some gross idea of their mutual engagements and the advantage of fulfilling them, but this only as far as their present and sensible interest required; for as to foresight they were utter strangers to it, and far from troubling their heads about a distant futurity, they scarce thought of the day following. Was a deer to be taken? Every one saw that to succeed he must faithfully stand to his post; but suppose a hare to have slipped by within reach of any one of them, it is not to be doubted but he pursued it without scruple, and when he had seized his prey never reproached himself with having made his companions miss theirs.

We may easily conceive that such an intercourse scarce required a more refined language than that of crows and monkeys, which flock together almost in the same manner. Inarticulate exclamations, a great many gestures, and some imitative sounds, must have been for a long time the universal language of mankind, and by joining to these in every country some articulate and conventional sounds, of which, as I have already hinted, it is not very easy to explain the institution, there arose particular languages, but rude, imperfect, and such nearly as are to be found at this day among several savage nations. My pen straightened by the rapidity of time, the abundance of things I have to say, and the almost insensible progress of the first improvements, flies like an arrow over numberless ages, for the slower the succession of events, the quicker I may allow myself to be in relating them.

At length, these first improvements enabled man to improve at a greater rate. Industry grew perfect in proportion as the mind became more enlightened. Men soon ceasing to fall asleep under the first tree, or take shelter in the first cavern, lit upon some hard and sharp kinds of stone resembling spades or hatchets, and employed them to dig the ground, cut down trees, and with the branches build huts, which they afterwards bethought themselves of plastering over with clay or dirt. This was the epoch of a first revolution, which produced the establishment and distinction of families, and which introduced a species of property, and along with it perhaps a thousand quarrels and battles. As the strongest however were probably the first to make themselves cabins, which they knew they were able to defend, we may conclude that the weak found it much shorter and safer to imitate than to attempt to dislodge them: and as to those, who were already provided with cabins, no one could have any great temptation to seize upon that of his neighbour, not so much because it did not belong to him, as because it could be of no service to him; and as besides to make himself master of it, he must expose himself to a very sharp conflict with the present occupiers.

The first developments of the heart were the effects of a new situation, which united husbands and wives, parents and children, under one roof; the habit of living together gave birth to the sweetest sentiments the human species is acquainted with, conjugal and paternal love. Every family became a little society, so much the more firmly united, as a mutual attachment and liberty were the only bonds of it; and it was now that the sexes, whose way of life had been hitherto the same, began to adopt different manners and customs. The women became more sedentary, and accustomed themselves to stay at home and look after the children, while the men rambled abroad in quest of subsistence for the whole family. The two sexes likewise by living a little more at their ease began to lose somewhat of their usual ferocity and sturdiness; but if on the one hand individuals became less able to engage separately with wild beasts, they on the other were more easily got together to make a common resistance against them.

In this new state of things, the simplicity and solitariness of man's life, the limitedness of his wants, and the instruments which he had invented to satisfy them, leaving him a great deal of leisure, he employed it to supply himself with several conveniences unknown to his ancestors; and this was the first yoke he inadvertently imposed upon himself, and the first source of mischief which he prepared for his children; for besides continuing in this manner to soften both body and mind, these conveniences having through use lost almost all their aptness to please, and even degenerated into real wants, the privation of them became far more intolerable than the possession of them had been agreeable; to lose them was a misfortune, to possess them no happiness.

Here we may a little better discover how the use of speech insensibly commences or improves in the bosom of every family, and may likewise from conjectures concerning the manner in which divers particular causes might have propagated language, and accelerated its progress by rendering it every day more and more necessary. Great inundations or earthquakes surrounded inhabited districts with water or precipices, portions of the continent were by revolutions of the globe torn off and split into islands. It is obvious that among men thus collected, and forced to live together, a common idiom must have started up much sooner, than among those who freely wandered through the forests of the main land. Thus it is very possible that the inhabitants of the islands formed in this manner, after their first essays in navigation, brought among us the use of speech; and it is very probable at least that society and languages commenced in islands and even acquired perfection there, before the inhabitants of the continent knew anything of either.

Everything now begins to wear a new aspect. Those who heretofore wandered through the woods, by taking to a more settled way of life, gradually flock together, coalesce into several separate bodies, and at length form in every country distinct nations, united in character and manners, not by any laws or regulations, but by an uniform manner of life, a sameness of provisions, and the common influence of the climate. A permanent neighborhood must at last infallibly create some connection between different families. The transitory commerce required by nature soon produced, among the youth of both sexes living in contiguous cabins, another kind of commerce, which besides being equally agreeable is rendered more durable by mutual intercourse. Men begin to consider different objects, and to make comparisons; they insensibly acquire ideas of merit and beauty, and these soon produce sentiments of preference. By seeing each other often they contract a habit, which makes it painful not to see each other always. Tender and agreeable sentiments steal into the soul, and are by the smallest opposition wound up into the most impetuous fury: Jealousy kindles with love; discord triumphs; and the gentlest of passions requires sacrifices of human blood to appease it.

In proportion as ideas and sentiments succeed each other, and the head and the heart exercise themselves, men continue to shake off their original wildness, and their connections become more intimate and extensive. They now begin to assemble round a great tree: singing and dancing, the genuine offspring of love and leisure, become the amusement or rather the occupation of the men and women, free from care, thus gathered together. Every one begins to survey the rest, and wishes to be surveyed himself; and public esteem acquires a value. He who sings or dances best; the handsomest, the strongest, the most dexterous, the most eloquent, comes to be the most respected: this was the first step towards inequality, and at the same time towards vice. From these first preferences there proceeded on one side vanity and contempt, on the other envy and shame; and the fermentation raised by these new leavens at length produced combinations fatal to happiness and innocence.

Men no sooner began to set a value upon each other, and know what esteem was, than each laid claim to it, and it was no longer safe for any man to refuse it to another. Hence the first duties of civility and politeness, even among savages; and hence every voluntary injury became an affront, as besides the mischief, which resulted from it as an injury, the party offended was sure to find in it a contempt for his person more intolerable than the mischief itself. It was thus that every man, punishing the contempt expressed for him by others in proportion to the value he set upon himself, the effects of revenge became terrible, and men learned to be sanguinary and cruel. Such precisely was the degree attained by most of the savage nations with whom we are acquainted. And it is for want of sufficiently distinguishing ideas, and observing at how great a distance these people were from the first state of nature, that so many authors have hastily concluded that man is naturally cruel, and requires a regular system of police to be reclaimed; whereas nothing can be more gentle than he in his primitive state, when placed by nature at an equal distance from the stupidity of brutes, and the pernicious good sense of civilized man; and equally confined by instinct and reason to the care of providing against the mischief which threatens him, he is withheld by natural compassion from doing any injury to others, so far from being ever so little prone even to return that which he has received. For according to the axiom of the wise Locke, Where there is no property, there can be no injury.

But we must take notice, that the society now formed and the relations now established among men required in them qualities different from those, which they derived from their primitive constitution; that as a sense of morality began to insinuate itself into human actions, and every man, before the enacting of laws, was the only judge and avenger of the injuries he had received, that goodness of heart suitable to the pure state of nature by no means suited infant society; that it was necessary punishments should become severer in the same proportion that the opportunities of offending became more frequent, and the dread of vengeance add strength to the too weak curb of the law. Thus, though men were become less patient, and natural compassion had already suffered some alteration, this period of the development of the human faculties, holding a just mean between the indolence of the primitive state, and the petulant activity of self-love, must have been the happiest and most durable epoch. The more we reflect on this state, the more convinced we shall be, that it was the least subject of any to revolutions, the best for man, and that nothing could have drawn him out of it but some fatal accident, which, for the public good, should never have happened. The example of the savages, most of whom have been found in this condition, seems to confirm that mankind was formed ever to remain in it, that this condition is the real youth of the world, and that all ulterior improvements have been so many steps, in appearance towards the perfection of individuals, but in fact towards the decrepitness of the species.

As long as men remained satisfied with their rustic cabins; as long as they confined themselves to the use of clothes made of the skins of other animals, and the use of thorns and fish-bones, in putting these skins together; as long as they continued to consider feathers and shells as sufficient ornaments, and to paint their bodies of different colours, to improve or ornament their bows and arrows, to form and scoop out with sharp-edged stones some little fishing boats, or clumsy instruments of music; in a word, as long as they undertook such works only as a single person could finish, and stuck to such arts as did not require the joint endeavours of several hands, they lived free, healthy, honest and happy, as much as their nature would admit, and continued to enjoy with each other all the pleasures of an independent intercourse; but from the moment one man began to stand in need of another's assistance; from the moment it appeared an advantage for one man to possess the quantity of provisions requisite for two, all equality vanished; property started up; labour became necessary; and boundless forests became smiling fields, which it was found necessary to water with human sweat, and in which slavery and misery were soon seen to sprout out and grow with the fruits of the earth.

Metallurgy and agriculture were the two arts whose invention produced this great revolution. With the poet, it is gold and silver, but with the philosopher it is iron and corn, which have civilized men, and ruined mankind. Accordingly both one and the other were unknown to the savages of America, who for that very reason have always continued savages; nay other nations seem to have continued in a state of barbarism, as long as they continued to exercise one only of these arts without the other; and perhaps one of the best reasons that can be assigned, why Europe has been, if not earlier, at least more constantly and better civilized than the other quarters of the world, is that she both abounds most in iron and is best qualified to produce corn.

It is a very difficult matter to tell how men came to know anything of iron, and the art of employing it: for we are not to suppose that they should of themselves think of digging it out of the mines, and preparing it for fusion, before they knew what could be the result of such a process. On the other hand, there is the less reason to attribute this discovery to any accidental fire, as mines are formed nowhere but in dry and barren places, and such as are bare of trees and plants, so that it looks as if nature had taken pains to keep from us so mischievous a secret. Nothing therefore remains but the extraordinary circumstance of some volcano, which, belching forth metallic substances ready fused, might have given the spectators a notion of imitating that operation of nature; and after all we must suppose them endued with an extraordinary stock of courage and foresight to undertake so painful a work, and have, at so great a distance, an eye to the advantages they might derive from it; qualities scarcely suitable but to heads more exercised, than those of such discoverers can be supposed to have been.

As to agriculture, the principles of it were known a long time before the practice of it took place, and it is hardly possible that men, constantly employed in drawing their subsistence from trees and plants, should not have early hit on the means employed by nature for the generation of vegetables; but in all probability it was very late before their industry took a turn that way, either because trees, which with their land and water game supplied them with sufficient food, did not require their attention; or because they did not know the use of corn; or because they had no instruments to cultivate it; or because they were destitute of foresight in regard to future necessities; or in fine, because they wanted means to hinder others from running away with the fruit of their labours. We may believe that on their becoming more industrious they began their agriculture by cultivating with sharp stones and pointed sticks a few pulse or roots about their cabins; and that it was a long time before they knew the method of preparing corn, and were provided with instruments necessary to raise it in large quantities; not to mention the necessity there is, in order to follow this occupation and sow lands, to consent to lose something at present to gain a great deal hereafter; a precaution very foreign to the turn of man's mind in a savage state, in which, as I have already taken notice, he can hardly foresee his wants from morning to night.

For this reason the invention of other arts must have been necessary to oblige mankind to apply to that of agriculture. As soon as men were wanted to fuse and forge iron, others were wanted to maintain them. The more hands were employed in manufactures, the fewer hands were left to provide subsistence for all, though the number of mouths to be supplied with food continued the same; and as some required commodities in exchange for their iron, the rest at last found out the method of making iron subservient to the multiplication of commodities. Hence on the one hand husbandry and agriculture, and on the other the art of working metals and of multiplying the uses of them.

To the tilling of the earth the distribution of it necessarily succeeded, and to property once acknowledged, the first rules of justice: for to secure every man his own, every man must have something. Moreover, as men began to extend their views to futurity, and all found themselves in possession of more or less goods capable of being lost, every one in particular had reason to fear, lest reprisals should be made on him for any injury he might do to others. This origin is so much the more natural, as it is impossible to conceive how property can flow from any other source but industry; for what can a man add but his labour to things which he has not made, in order to acquire a property in them? 'Tis the labour of the hands alone, which giving the husbandman a title to the produce of the land he has tilled gives him a title to the land itself, at least till he has gathered in the fruits of it, and so on from year to year; and this enjoyment forming a continued possession is easily transformed into a property. The ancients, says Grotius, by giving to Ceres the epithet of Legislatrix, and to a festival celebrated in her honour the name of Thesmorphoria, insinuated that the distribution of lands produced a new kind of right; that is, the right of property different from that which results from the law of nature.

Things thus circumstanced might have remained equal, if men's talents had been equal, and if, for instance, the use of iron, and the consumption of commodities had always held an exact proportion to each other; but as this proportion had no support, it was soon broken. The man that had most strength performed most labour; the most dexterous turned his labour to best account; the most ingenious found out methods of lessening his labour; the husbandman required more iron, or the smith more corn, and while both worked equally, one earned a great deal by his labour, while the other could scarce live by his. It is thus that natural inequality insensibly unfolds itself with that arising from a variety of combinations, and that the difference among men, developed by the difference of their circumstances, becomes more sensible, more permanent in its effects, and begins to influence in the same proportion the condition of private persons.

Things once arrived at this period, it is an easy matter to imagine the rest. I shall not stop to describe the successive inventions of other arts, the progress of language, the trial and employments of talents, the inequality of fortunes, the use or abuse of riches, nor all the details which follow these, and which every one may easily supply. I shall just give a glance at mankind placed in this new order of things.

Behold then all our faculties developed; our memory and imagination at work, self-love interested; reason rendered active; and the mind almost arrived at the utmost bounds of that perfection it is capable of. Behold all our natural qualities put in motion; the rank and condition of every man established, not only as to the quantum of property and the power of serving or hurting others, but likewise as to genius, beauty, strength or address, merit or talents; and as these were the only qualities which could command respect, it was found necessary to have or at least to affect them. It was requisite for men to be thought what they really were not. To be and to appear became two very different things, and from this distinction sprang pomp and knavery, and all the vices which form their train. On the other hand, man, heretofore free and independent, was now in consequence of a multitude of new wants brought under subjection, as it were, to all nature, and especially to his fellows, whose slave in some sense he became even by becoming their master; if rich, he stood in need of their services, if poor, of their assistance; even mediocrity itself could not enable him to do without them. He must therefore have been continually at work to interest them in his happiness, and make them, if not really, at least apparently find their advantage in labouring for his: this rendered him sly and artful in his dealings with some, imperious and cruel in his dealings with others, and laid him under the necessity of using ill all those whom he stood in need of, as often as he could not awe them into a compliance with his will, and did not find it his interest to purchase it at the expense of real services. In fine, an insatiable ambition, the rage of raising their relative fortunes, not so much through real necessity, as to over-top others, inspire all men with a wicked inclination to injure each other, and with a secret jealousy so much the more dangerous, as to carry its point with the greater security, it often puts on the face of benevolence. In a word, sometimes nothing was to be seen but a contention of endeavours on the one hand, and an opposition of interests on the other, while a secret desire of thriving at the expense of others constantly prevailed. Such were the first effects of property, and the inseparable attendants of infant inequality.

Riches, before the invention of signs to represent them, could scarce consist in anything but lands and cattle, the only real goods which men can possess. But when estates increased so much in number and in extent as to take in whole countries and touch each other, it became impossible for one man to aggrandise himself but at the expense of some other; and the supernumerary inhabitants, who were too weak or too indolent to make such acquisitions in their turn, impoverished without losing anything, because while everything about them changed they alone remained the same, were obliged to receive or force their subsistence from the hands of the rich. And hence began to flow, according to the different characters of each, domination and slavery, or violence and rapine. The rich on their side scarce began to taste the pleasure of commanding, when they preferred it to every other; and making use of their old slaves to acquire new ones, they no longer thought of anything but subduing and enslaving their neighbours; like those ravenous wolves, who having once tasted human flesh, despise every other food, and devour nothing but men for the future.

It is thus that the most powerful or the most wretched, respectively considering their power and wretchedness as a kind of title to the substance of others, even equivalent to that of property, the equality once broken was followed by the most shocking disorders. It is thus that the usurpations of the rich, the pillagings of the poor, and the unbridled passions of all, by stifling the cries of natural compassion, and the as yet feeble voice of justice, rendered man avaricious, wicked and ambitious. There arose between the title of the strongest, and that of the first occupier a perpetual conflict, which always ended in battery and bloodshed. Infant society became a scene of the most horrible warfare: Mankind thus debased and harassed, and no longer able to retreat, or renounce the unhappy acquisitions it had made; labouring, in short merely to its confusion by the abuse of those faculties, which in themselves do it so much honour, brought itself to the very brink of ruin and destruction.

Attonitus novitate mali, divesque miserque, Effugere optat opes; et quoe modo voverat, odit.

But it is impossible that men should not sooner or later have made reflections on so wretched a situation, and upon the calamities with which they were overwhelmed. The rich in particular must have soon perceived how much they suffered by a perpetual war, of which they alone supported all the expense, and in which, though all risked life, they alone risked any substance. Besides, whatever colour they might pretend to give their usurpations, they sufficiently saw that these usurpations were in the main founded upon false and precarious titles, and that what they had acquired by mere force, others could again by mere force wrest out of their hands, without leaving them the least room to complain of such a proceeding. Even those, who owed all their riches to their own industry, could scarce ground their acquisitions upon a better title. It availed them nothing to say, 'Twas I built this wall; I acquired this spot by my labour. Who traced it out for you, another might object, and what right have you to expect payment at our expense for doing that we did not oblige you to do? Don't you know that numbers of your brethren perish, or suffer grievously for want of what you possess more than suffices nature, and that you should have had the express and unanimous consent of mankind to appropriate to yourself of their common, more than was requisite for your private subsistence? Destitute of solid reasons to justify, and sufficient force to defend himself; crushing individuals with ease, but with equal ease crushed by numbers; one against all, and unable, on account of mutual jealousies, to unite with his equals against banditti united by the common hopes of pillage; the rich man, thus pressed by necessity, at last conceived the deepest project that ever entered the human mind: this was to employ in his favour the very forces that attacked him, to make allies of his enemies, to inspire them with other maxims, and make them adopt other institutions as favourable to his pretensions, as the law of nature was unfavourable to them.

With this view, after laying before his neighbours all the horrors of a situation, which armed them all one against another, which rendered their possessions as burdensome as their wants were intolerable, and in which no one could expect any safety either in poverty or riches, he easily invented specious arguments to bring them over to his purpose. "Let us unite," said he, "to secure the weak from oppression, restrain the ambitious, and secure to every man the possession of what belongs to him: Let us form rules of justice and peace, to which all may be obliged to conform, which shall not except persons, but may in some sort make amends for the caprice of fortune, by submitting alike the powerful and the weak to the observance of mutual duties. In a word, instead of turning our forces against ourselves, let us collect them into a sovereign power, which may govern us by wise laws, may protect and defend all the members of the association, repel common enemies, and maintain a perpetual concord and harmony among us."

Much fewer words of this kind were sufficient to draw in a parcel of rustics, whom it was an easy matter to impose upon, who had besides too many quarrels among themselves to live without arbiters, and too much avarice and ambition to live long without masters. All offered their necks to the yoke in hopes of securing their liberty; for though they had sense enough to perceive the advantages of a political constitution, they had not experience enough to see beforehand the dangers of it; those among them, who were best qualified to foresee abuses, were precisely those who expected to benefit by them; even the soberest judged it requisite to sacrifice one part of their liberty to ensure the other, as a man, dangerously wounded in any of his limbs, readily parts with it to save the rest of his body.

Such was, or must have been, had man been left to himself, the origin of society and of the laws, which increased the fetters of the weak, and the strength of the rich; irretrievably destroyed natural liberty, fixed for ever the laws of property and inequality; changed an artful usurpation into an irrevocable title; and for the benefit of a few ambitious individuals subjected the rest of mankind to perpetual labour, servitude, and misery. We may easily conceive how the establishment of a single society rendered that of all the rest absolutely necessary, and how, to make head against united forces, it became necessary for the rest of mankind to unite in their turn. Societies once formed in this manner, soon multiplied or spread to such a degree, as to cover the face of the earth; and not to leave a corner in the whole universe, where a man could throw off the yoke, and withdraw his head from under the often ill-conducted sword which he saw perpetually hanging over it. The civil law being thus become the common rule of citizens, the law of nature no longer obtained but among the different societies, in which, under the name of the law of nations, it was qualified by some tacit conventions to render commerce possible, and supply the place of natural compassion, which, losing by degrees all that influence over societies which it originally had over individuals, no longer exists but in some great souls, who consider themselves as citizens of the world, and forcing the imaginary barriers that separate people from people, after the example of the Sovereign Being from whom we all derive our existence, make the whole human race the object of their benevolence.

Political bodies, thus remaining in a state of nature among themselves, soon experienced the inconveniences which had obliged individuals to quit it; and this state became much more fatal to these great bodies, than it had been before to the individuals which now composed them. Hence those national wars, those battles, those murders, those reprisals, which make nature shudder and shock reason; hence all those horrible prejudices, which make it a virtue and an honour to shed human blood. The worthiest men learned to consider the cutting the throats of their fellows as a duty; at length men began to butcher each other by thousands without knowing for what; and more murders were committed in a single action, and more horrible disorders at the taking of a single town, than had been committed in the state of nature during ages together upon the whole face of the earth. Such are the first effects we may conceive to have arisen from the division of mankind into different societies. Let us return to their institution.

I know that several writers have assigned other origins of political society; as for instance, the conquests of the powerful, or the union of the weak; and it is no matter which of these causes we adopt in regard to what I am going to establish; that, however, which I have just laid down, seems to me the most natural, for the following reasons: First, because, in the first case, the right of conquest being in fact no right at all, it could not serve as a foundation for any other right, the conqueror and the conquered ever remaining with respect to each other in a state of war, unless the conquered, restored to the full possession of their liberty, should freely choose their conqueror for their chief. Till then, whatever capitulations might have been made between them, as these capitulations were founded upon violence, and of course de facto null and void, there could not have existed in this hypothesis either a true society, or a political body, or any other law but that of the strongest. Second, because these words strong and weak, are ambiguous in the second case; for during the interval between the establishment of the right of property or prior occupation and that of political government, the meaning of these terms is better expressed by the words poor and rich, as before the establishment of laws men in reality had no other means of reducing their equals, but by invading the property of these equals, or by parting with some of their own property to them. Third, because the poor having nothing but their liberty to lose, it would have been the height of madness in them to give up willingly the only blessing they had left without obtaining some consideration for it: whereas the rich being sensible, if I may say so, in every part of their possessions, it was much easier to do them mischief, and therefore more incumbent upon them to guard against it; and because, in fine, it is but reasonable to suppose, that a thing has been invented by him to whom it could be of service rather than by him to whom it must prove detrimental.

Government in its infancy had no regular and permanent form. For want of a sufficient fund of philosophy and experience, men could see no further than the present inconveniences, and never thought of providing remedies for future ones, but in proportion as they arose. In spite of all the labours of the wisest legislators, the political state still continued imperfect, because it was in a manner the work of chance; and, as the foundations of it were ill laid, time, though sufficient to discover its defects and suggest the remedies for them, could never mend its original vices. Men were continually repairing; whereas, to erect a good edifice, they should have begun as Lycurgus did at Sparta, by clearing the area, and removing the old materials. Society at first consisted merely of some general conventions which all the members bound themselves to observe, and for the performance of which the whole body became security to every individual. Experience was necessary to show the great weakness of such a constitution, and how easy it was for those, who infringed it, to escape the conviction or chastisement of faults, of which the public alone was to be both the witness and the judge;

the laws could not fail of being eluded a thousand ways; inconveniences and disorders could not but multiply continually, till it was at last found necessary to think of committing to private persons the dangerous trust of public authority, and to magistrates the care of enforcing obedience to the people: for to say that chiefs were elected before confederacies were formed, and that the ministers of the laws existed before the laws themselves, is a supposition too ridiculous to deserve I should seriously refute it.

It would be equally unreasonable to imagine that men at first threw themselves into the arms of an absolute master, without any conditions or consideration on his side; and that the first means contrived by jealous and unconquered men for their common safety was to run hand over head into slavery. In fact, why did they give themselves superiors, if it was not to be defended by them against oppression, and protected in their lives, liberties, and properties, which are in a manner the constitutional elements of their being? Now in the relations between man and man, the worst that can happen to one man being to see himself at the discretion of another, would it not have been contrary to the dictates of good sense to begin by making over to a chief the only things for the preservation of which they stood in need of his assistance? What equivalent could he have offered them for so fine a privilege? And had he presumed to exact it on pretense of defending them, would he not have immediately received the answer in the apologue? What worse treatment can we expect from an enemy? It is therefore past dispute, and indeed a fundamental maxim of political law, that people gave themselves chiefs to defend their liberty and not be enslaved by them. If we have a prince, said Pliny to Trajan, it is in order that he may keep us from having a master.

Political writers argue in regard to the love of liberty with the same philosophy that philosophers do in regard to the state of nature; by the things they see they judge of things very different which they have never seen, and they attribute to men a natural inclination to slavery, on account of the patience with which the slaves within their notice carry the yoke; not reflecting that it is with liberty as with innocence and virtue, the value of which is not known but by those who possess them, though the relish for them is lost with the things themselves. I know the charms of your country, said Brasidas to a satrap who was comparing the life of the Spartans with that of the Persepolites; but you can not know the pleasures of mine.

As an unbroken courser erects his mane, paws the ground, and rages at the bare sight of the bit, while a trained horse patiently suffers both whip and spur, just so the barbarian will never reach his neck to the yoke which civilized man carries without murmuring but prefers the most stormy liberty to a calm subjection. It is not therefore by the servile disposition of enslaved nations that we must judge of the natural dispositions of man for or against slavery, but by the prodigies done by every free people to secure themselves from oppression. I know that the first are constantly crying up that peace and tranquillity they enjoy in their irons, and that _miserrimam servitutem pacem appellant_: but when I see the others sacrifice pleasures, peace, riches, power, and even life itself to the preservation of that single jewel so much slighted by those who have lost it; when I see free-born animals through a natural abhorrence of captivity dash their brains out against the bars of their prison; when I see multitudes of naked savages despise European pleasures, and brave hunger, fire and sword, and death itself to preserve their independency; I feel that it belongs not to slaves to argue concerning liberty.

As to paternal authority, from which several have derived absolute government and every other mode of society, it is sufficient, without having recourse to Locke and Sidney, to observe that nothing in the world differs more from the cruel spirit of despotism that the gentleness of that authority, which looks more to the advantage of him who obeys than to the utility of him who commands; that by the law of nature the father continues master of his child no longer than the child stands in need of his assistance; that after that term they become equal, and that then the son, entirely independent of the father, owes him no obedience, but only respect. Gratitude is indeed a duty which we are bound to pay, but which benefactors can not exact. Instead of saying that civil society is derived from paternal authority, we should rather say that it is to the former that the latter owes its principal force: No one individual was acknowledged as the father of several other individuals, till they settled about him. The father's goods, which he can indeed dispose of as he pleases, are the ties which hold his children to their dependence upon him, and he may divide his substance among them in proportion as they shall have deserved his attention by a continual deference to his commands. Now the subjects of a despotic chief, far from having any such favour to expect from him, as both themselves and all they have are his property, or at least are considered by him as such, are obliged to receive as a favour what he relinquishes to them of their own property. He does them justice when he strips them; he treats them with mercy when he suffers them to live. By continuing in this manner to compare facts with right, we should discover as little solidity as truth in the voluntary establishment of tyranny; and it would be a hard matter to prove the validity of a contract which was binding only on one side, in which one of the parties should stake everything and the other nothing, and which could turn out to the prejudice of him alone who had bound himself.

This odious system is even, at this day, far from being that of wise and good monarchs, and especially of the kings of France, as may be seen by divers passages in their edicts, and particularly by that of a celebrated piece published in 1667 in the name and by the orders of Louis XIV. "Let it therefore not be said that the sovereign is not subject to the laws of his realm, since, that he is, is a maxim of the law of nations which flattery has sometimes attacked, but which good princes have always defended as the tutelary divinity of their realms. How much more reasonable is it to say with the sage Plato, that the perfect happiness of a state consists in the subjects obeying their prince, the prince obeying the laws, and the laws being equitable and always directed to the good of the public?" I shall not stop to consider, if, liberty being the most noble faculty of man, it is not degrading one's nature, reducing one's self to the level of brutes, who are the slaves of instinct, and even offending the author of one's being, to renounce without reserve the most precious of his gifts, and submit to the commission of all the crimes he has forbid us, merely to gratify a mad or a cruel master; and if this sublime artist ought to be more irritated at seeing his work destroyed than at seeing it dishonoured. I shall only ask what right those, who were not afraid thus to degrade themselves, could have to subject their dependants to the same ignominy, and renounce, in the name of their posterity, blessings for which it is not indebted to their liberality, and without which life itself must appear a burthen to all those who are worthy to live.

Puffendorf says that, as we can transfer our property from one to another by contracts and conventions, we may likewise divest ourselves of our liberty in favour of other men. This, in my opinion, is a very poor way of arguing; for, in the first place, the property I cede to another becomes by such cession a thing quite foreign to me, and the abuse of which can no way affect me; but it concerns me greatly that my liberty is not abused, and I can not, without incurring the guilt of the crimes I may be forced to commit, expose myself to become the instrument of any. Besides, the right of property being of mere human convention and institution, every man may dispose as he pleases of what he possesses: But the case is otherwise with regard to the essential gifts of nature, such as life and liberty, which every man is permitted to enjoy, and of which it is doubtful at least whether any man has a right to divest himself: By giving up the one, we degrade our being; by giving up the other we annihilate it as much as it is our power to do so; and as no temporal enjoyments can indemnify us for the loss of either, it would be at once offending both nature and reason to renounce them for any consideration. But though we could transfer our liberty as we do our substance, the difference would be very great with regard to our children, who enjoy our substance but by a cession of our right; whereas liberty being a blessing, which as men they hold from nature, their parents have no right to strip them of it; so that as to establish slavery it was necessary to do violence to nature, so it was necessary to alter nature to perpetuate such a right; and the jurisconsults, who have gravely pronounced that the child of a slave comes a slave into the world, have in other words decided, that a man does not come a man into the world.

It therefore appears to me incontestably true, that not only governments did not begin by arbitrary power, which is but the corruption and extreme term of government, and at length brings it back to the law of the strongest, against which governments were at first the remedy, but even that, allowing they had commenced in this manner, such power being illegal in itself could never have served as a foundation to the rights of society, nor of course to the inequality of institution.

I shall not now enter upon the inquiries which still remain to be made into the nature of the fundamental pacts of every kind of government, but, following the common opinion, confine myself in this place to the establishment of the political body as a real contract between the multitude and the chiefs elected by it. A contract by which both parties oblige themselves to the observance of the laws that are therein stipulated, and form the bands of their union. The multitude having, on occasion of the social relations between them, concentered all their wills in one person, all the articles, in regard to which this will explains itself, become so many fundamental laws, which oblige without exception all the members of the state, and one of which laws regulates the choice and the power of the magistrates appointed to look to the execution of the rest. This power extends to everything that can maintain the constitution, but extends to nothing that can alter it. To this power are added honours, that may render the laws and the ministers of them respectable; and the persons of the ministers are distinguished by certain prerogatives, which may make them amends for the great fatigues inseparable from a good administration. The magistrate, on his side, obliges himself not to use the power with which he is intrusted but conformably to the intention of his constituents, to maintain every one of them in the peaceable possession of his property, and upon all occasions prefer the good of the public to his own private interest.

Before experience had demonstrated, or a thorough knowledge of the human heart had pointed out, the abuses inseparable from such a constitution, it must have appeared so much the more perfect, as those appointed to look to its preservation were themselves most concerned therein; for magistracy and its rights being built solely on the fundamental laws, as soon as these ceased to exist, the magistrates would cease to be lawful, the people would no longer be bound to obey them, and, as the essence of the state did not consist in the magistrates but in the laws, the members of it would immediately become entitled to their primitive and natural liberty.

A little reflection would afford us new arguments in confirmation of this truth, and the nature of the contract might alone convince us that it can not be irrevocable: for if there was no superior power capable of guaranteeing the fidelity of the contracting parties and of obliging them to fulfil their mutual engagements, they would remain sole judges in their own cause, and each of them would always have a right to renounce the contract, as soon as he discovered that the other had broke the conditions of it, or that these conditions ceased to suit his private convenience. Upon this principle, the right of abdication may probably be founded. Now, to consider as we do nothing but what is human in this institution, if the magistrate, who has all the power in his own hands, and who appropriates to himself all the advantages of the contract, has notwithstanding a right to divest himself of his authority; how much a better right must the people, who pay for all the faults of its chief, have to renounce their dependence upon him. But the shocking dissensions and disorders without number, which would be the necessary consequence of so dangerous a privilege, show more than anything else how much human governments stood in need of a more solid basis than that of mere reason, and how necessary it was for the public tranquillity, that the will of the Almighty should interpose to give to sovereign authority, a sacred and inviolable character, which should deprive subjects of the mischievous right to dispose of it to whom they pleased. If mankind had received no other advantages from religion, this alone would be sufficient to make them adopt and cherish it, since it is the means of saving more blood than fanaticism has been the cause of spilling. But to resume the thread of our hypothesis.

The various forms of government owe their origin to the various degrees of inequality between the members, at the time they first coalesced into a political body. Where a man happened to be eminent for power, for virtue, for riches, or for credit, he became sole magistrate, and the state assumed a monarchical form; if many of pretty equal eminence out-topped all the rest, they were jointly elected, and this election produced an aristocracy; those, between whose fortune or talents there happened to be no such disproportion, and who had deviated less from the state of nature, retained in common the supreme administration, and formed a democracy. Time demonstrated which of these forms suited mankind best. Some remained altogether subject to the laws; others soon bowed their necks to masters. The former laboured to preserve their liberty; the latter thought of nothing but invading that of their neighbours, jealous at seeing others enjoy a blessing which themselves had lost. In a word, riches and conquest fell to the share of the one, and virtue and happiness to that of the other.

In these various modes of government the offices at first were all elective; and when riches did not preponderate, the preference was given to merit, which gives a natural ascendant, and to age, which is the parent of deliberateness in council, and experience in execution. The ancients among the Hebrews, the Geronts of Sparta, the Senate of Rome, nay, the very etymology of our word seigneur, show how much gray hairs were formerly respected. The oftener the choice fell upon old men, the oftener it became necessary to repeat it, and the more the trouble of such repetitions became sensible; electioneering took place; factions arose; the parties contracted ill blood; civil wars blazed forth; the lives of the citizens were sacrificed to the pretended happiness of the state; and things at last came to such a pass, as to be ready to relapse into their primitive confusion. The ambition of the principal men induced them to take advantage of these circumstances to perpetuate the hitherto temporary charges in their families; the people already inured to dependence, accustomed to ease and the conveniences of life, and too much enervated to break their fetters, consented to the increase of their slavery for the sake of securing their tranquillity; and it is thus that chiefs, become hereditary, contracted the habit of considering magistracies as a family estate, and themselves as proprietors of those communities, of which at first they were but mere officers; to call their fellow-citizens their slaves; to look upon them, like so many cows or sheep, as a part of their substance; and to style themselves the peers of Gods, and Kings of Kings.

By pursuing the progress of inequality in these different revolutions, we shall discover that the establishment of laws and of the right of property was the first term of it; the institution of magistrates the second; and the third and last the changing of legal into arbitrary power; so that the different states of rich and poor were authorized by the first epoch; those of powerful and weak by the second; and by the third those of master and slave, which formed the last degree of inequality, and the term in which all the rest at last end, till new revolutions entirely dissolve the government, or bring it back nearer to its legal constitution.

To conceive the necessity of this progress, we are not so much to consider the motives for the establishment of political bodies, as the forms these bodies assume in their administration; and the inconveniences with which they are essentially attended; for those vices, which render social institutions necessary, are the same which render the abuse of such institutions unavoidable; and as (Sparta alone excepted, whose laws chiefly regarded the education of children, and where Lycurgus established such manners and customs, as in a great measure made laws needless,) the laws, in general less strong than the passions, restrain men without changing them; it would be no hard matter to prove that every government, which carefully guarding against all alteration and corruption should scrupulously comply with the ends of its institution, was unnecessarily instituted; and that a country, where no one either eluded the laws, or made an ill use of magistracy, required neither laws nor magistrates.

Political distinctions are necessarily attended with civil distinctions. The inequality between the people and the chiefs increase so fast as to be soon felt by the private members, and appears among them in a thousand shapes according to their passions, their talents, and the circumstances of affairs. The magistrate can not usurp any illegal power without making himself creatures, with whom he must divide it. Besides, the citizens of a free state suffer themselves to be oppressed merely in proportion as, hurried on by a blind ambition, and looking rather below than above them, they come to love authority more than independence. When they submit to fetters, 'tis only to be the better able to fetter others in their turn. It is no easy matter to make him obey, who does not wish to command; and the most refined policy would find it impossible to subdue those men, who only desire to be independent; but inequality easily gains ground among base and ambitious souls, ever ready to run the risks of fortune, and almost indifferent whether they command or obey, as she proves either favourable or adverse to them. Thus then there must have been a time, when the eyes of the people were bewitched to such a degree, that their rulers needed only to have said to the most pitiful wretch, "Be great you and all your posterity," to make him immediately appear great in the eyes of every one as well as in his own; and his descendants took still more upon them, in proportion to their removes from him: the more distant and uncertain the cause, the greater the effect; the longer line of drones a family produced, the more illustrious it was reckoned.

Were this a proper place to enter into details, I could easily explain in what manner inequalities in point of credit and authority become unavoidable among private persons the moment that, united into one body, they are obliged to compare themselves one with another, and to note the differences which they find in the continual use every man must make of his neighbour. These differences are of several kinds; but riches, nobility or rank, power and personal merit, being in general the principal distinctions, by which men in society measure each other, I could prove that the harmony or conflict between these different forces is the surest indication of the good or bad original constitution of any state: I could make it appear that, as among these four kinds of inequality, personal qualities are the source of all the rest, riches is that in which they ultimately terminate, because, being the most immediately useful to the prosperity of individuals, and the most easy to communicate, they are made use of to purchase every other distinction. By this observation we are enabled to judge with tolerable exactness, how much any people has deviated from its primitive institution, and what steps it has still to make to the extreme term of corruption. I could show how much this universal desire of reputation, of honours, of preference, with which we are all devoured, exercises and compares our talents and our forces: how much it excites and multiplies our passions; and, by creating an universal competition, rivalship, or rather enmity among men, how many disappointments, successes, and catastrophes of every kind it daily causes among the innumerable pretenders whom it engages in the same career. I could show that it is to this itch of being spoken of, to this fury of distinguishing ourselves which seldom or never gives us a moment's respite, that we owe both the best and the worst things among us, our virtues and our vices, our sciences and our errors, our conquerors and our philosophers; that is to say, a great many bad things to a very few good ones. I could prove, in short, that if we behold a handful of rich and powerful men seated on the pinnacle of fortune and greatness, while the crowd grovel in obscurity and want, it is merely because the first prize what they enjoy but in the same degree that others want it, and that, without changing their condition, they would cease to be happy the minute the people ceased to be miserable.

But these details would alone furnish sufficient matter for a more considerable work, in which might be weighed the advantages and disadvantages of every species of government, relatively to the rights of man in a state of nature, and might likewise be unveiled all the different faces under which inequality has appeared to this day, and may hereafter appear to the end of time, according to the nature of these several governments, and the revolutions time must unavoidably occasion in them. We should then see the multitude oppressed by domestic tyrants in consequence of those very precautions taken by them to guard against foreign masters. We should see oppression increase continually without its being ever possible for the oppressed to know where it would stop, nor what lawful means they had left to check its progress. We should see the rights of citizens, and the liberties of nations extinguished by slow degrees, and the groans, and protestations and appeals of the weak treated as seditious murmurings. We should see policy confine to a mercenary portion of the people the honour of defending the common cause. We should see imposts made necessary by such measures, the disheartened husbandman desert his field even in time of peace, and quit the plough to take up the sword. We should see fatal and whimsical rules laid down concerning the point of honour. We should see the champions of their country sooner or later become her enemies, and perpetually holding their poniards to the breasts of their fellow citizens. Nay, the time would come when they might be heard to say to the oppressor of their country:

Pectore si fratris gladium juguloque parentis Condere me jubeas, gravidoeque in viscera partu Conjugis, in vita peragam tamen omnia dextra.

From the vast inequality of conditions and fortunes, from the great variety of passions and of talents, of useless arts, of pernicious arts, of frivolous sciences, would issue clouds of prejudices equally contrary to reason, to happiness, to virtue. We should see the chiefs foment everything that tends to weaken men formed into societies by dividing them; everything that, while it gives society an air of apparent harmony, sows in it the seeds of real division; everything that can inspire the different orders with mutual distrust and hatred by an opposition of their rights and interest, and of course strengthen that power which contains them all.

'Tis from the bosom of this disorder and these revolutions, that despotism gradually rearing up her hideous crest, and devouring in every part of the state all that still remained sound and untainted, would at last issue to trample upon the laws and the people, and establish herself upon the ruins of the republic. The times immediately preceding this last alteration would be times of calamity and trouble: but at last everything would be swallowed up by the monster; and the people would no longer have chiefs or laws, but only tyrants. At this fatal period all regard to virtue and manners would likewise disappear; for despotism, _cui ex honesto nulla est spes_, tolerates no other master, wherever it reigns; the moment it speaks, probity and duty lose all their influence, and the blindest obedience is the only virtue the miserable slaves have left them to practise.

This is the last term of inequality, the extreme point which closes the circle and meets that from which we set out. 'Tis here that all private men return to their primitive equality, because they are no longer of any account; and that, the subjects having no longer any law but that of their master, nor the master any other law but his passions, all notions of good and principles of justice again disappear. 'Tis here that everything returns to the sole law of the strongest, and of course to a new state of nature different from that with which we began, in as much as the first was the state of nature in its purity, and the last the consequence of excessive corruption. There is, in other respects, so little difference between these two states, and the contract of government is so much dissolved by despotism, that the despot is no longer master than he continues the strongest, and that, as soon as his slaves can expel him, they may do it without his having the least right to complain of their using him ill. The insurrection, which ends in the death or despotism of a sultan, is as juridical an act as any by which the day before he disposed of the lives and fortunes of his subjects. Force alone upheld him, force alone overturns him. Thus all things take place and succeed in their natural order; and whatever may be the upshot of these hasty and frequent revolutions, no one man has reason to complain of another's injustice, but only of his own indiscretion or bad fortune.

By thus discovering and following the lost and forgotten tracks, by which man from the natural must have arrived at the civil state; by restoring, with the intermediate positions which I have been just indicating, those which want of leisure obliges me to suppress, or which my imagination has not suggested, every attentive reader must unavoidably be struck at the immense space which separates these two states. 'Tis in this slow succession of things he may meet with the solution of an infinite number of problems in morality and politics, which philosophers are puzzled to solve. He will perceive that, the mankind of one age not being the mankind of another, the reason why Diogenes could not find a man was, that he sought among his cotemporaries the man of an earlier period: Cato, he will then see, fell with Rome and with liberty, because he did not suit the age in which he lived; and the greatest of men served only to astonish that world, which would have cheerfully obeyed him, had he come into it five hundred years earlier. In a word, he will find himself in a condition to understand how the soul and the passions of men by insensible alterations change as it were their nature; how it comes to pass, that at the long run our wants and our pleasures change objects; that, original man vanishing by degrees, society no longer offers to our inspection but an assemblage of artificial men and factitious passions, which are the work of all these new relations, and have no foundation in nature. Reflection teaches us nothing on that head, but what experience perfectly confirms. Savage man and civilised man differ so much at bottom in point of inclinations and passions, that what constitutes the supreme happiness of the one would reduce the other to despair. The first sighs for nothing but repose and liberty;

he desires only to live, and to be exempt from labour; nay, the ataraxy of the most confirmed Stoic falls short of his consummate indifference for every other object. On the contrary, the citizen always in motion, is perpetually sweating and toiling, and racking his brains to find out occupations still more laborious: He continues a drudge to his last minute; nay, he courts death to be able to live, or renounces life to acquire immortality. He cringes to men in power whom he hates, and to rich men whom he despises; he sticks at nothing to have the honour of serving them; he is not ashamed to value himself on his own weakness and the protection they afford him; and proud of his chains, he speaks with disdain of those who have not the honour of being the partner of his bondage. What a spectacle must the painful and envied labours of an European minister of state form in the eyes of a Caribbean! How many cruel deaths would not this indolent savage prefer to such a horrid life, which very often is not even sweetened by the pleasure of doing good? But to see the drift of so many cares, his mind should first have affixed some meaning to these words power and reputation; he should be apprised that there are men who consider as something the looks of the rest of mankind, who know how to be happy and satisfied with themselves on the testimony of others sooner than upon their own. In fact, the real source of all those differences, is that the savage lives within himself, whereas the citizen, constantly beside himself, knows only how to live in the opinion of others; insomuch that it is, if I may say so, merely from their judgment that he derives the consciousness of his own existence. It is foreign to my subject to show how this disposition engenders so much indifference for good and evil, notwithstanding so many and such fine discourses of morality; how everything, being reduced to appearances, becomes mere art and mummery; honour, friendship, virtue, and often vice itself, which we at last learn the secret to boast of; how, in short, ever inquiring of others what we are, and never daring to question ourselves on so delicate a point, in the midst of so much philosophy, humanity, and politeness, and so many sublime maxims, we have nothing to show for ourselves but a deceitful and frivolous exterior, honour without virtue, reason without wisdom, and pleasure without happiness. It is sufficient that I have proved that this is not the original condition of man, and that it is merely the spirit of society, and the inequality which society engenders, that thus change and transform all our natural inclinations.

I have endeavoured to exhibit the origin and progress of inequality, the institution and abuse of political societies, as far as these things are capable of being deduced from the nature of man by the mere light of reason, and independently of those sacred maxims which give to the sovereign authority the sanction of divine right. It follows from this picture, that as there is scarce any inequality among men in a state of nature, all that which we now behold owes its force and its growth to the development of our faculties and the improvement of our understanding, and at last becomes permanent and lawful by the establishment of property and of laws. It likewise follows that moral inequality, authorised by any right that is merely positive, clashes with natural right, as often as it does not combine in the same proportion with physical inequality: a distinction which sufficiently determines, what we are able to think in that respect of that kind of inequality which obtains in all civilised nations, since it is evidently against the law of nature that infancy should command old age, folly conduct wisdom, and a handful of men should be ready to choke with superfluities, while the famished multitude want the commonest necessaries of life.

###

www.ingramcontent.com/pod-product-compliance
Lightning Source LLC
Chambersburg PA
CBHW072050040426
42447CB00012BB/3085